LEGEND
OF
THE
UINTAS

Daniel Hance Page

This book is a work of fiction.
Places, events, and situations in
this story are purely fictional. Any
resemblance to actual persons,
living or dead, is coincidental.

ISBN: 1-4033-1138-2 (e-book)
ISBN: 1-4033-1139-0 (Paperback)

This book is printed on acid free
paper.

1stBooks - rev. 06/04/02

"When we try to pick out anything by itself, we find it hitched to everything else in the universe."

John Muir, 1911.

For

the people with whom I have enjoyed Belleair Beach. We lived beside the sea and realized we were part of it.

ONE

MECEDAH

The old chief, Mecedah, had lost the respect of the people in his village. His village had been located south of the mountains that would later be known as the Uintas in northeastern Utah.

Spain's expansion into the New World of the Americas was marked by cruelty to the land's first inhabitants, the Indian people. Spain's pillaging of the New World robbed the Indian nations and sent Indian gold on ships back to Spain. These attacks reached Acoma Pueblo, or Sky City, in 1598. During this year, most of the town's inhabitants were massacred, leaving about six

1

hundred to, ironically, build a church.

Attacks continued. In 1778, Mecedah's father was killed defending his village located south of the Uintas. Many men from the village were enslaved to work at the gold mine in the mountains later called the Uintas. Mecedah was not forgiven by the people for seeming to do very little to defend the village. Actually he had done as much as he could. The people did not know that the battle had kindled a fire in Mececah and this flame burned all his life.

He collected weapons, giving them to men for a day when there would be another battle. He also used his friend, the river.

From the river, Mecedah took fish. He hunted along the broad stream's banks to acquire other abundant food in addition to furs. He shot mule deer, elk and moose. He also trapped beavers, bears and mountain lions. Occasionally, he surprised and shot an antelope.

Although meat and furs were shared with scattered members of the village, Mecedah continued to receive little respect. Sharing was expected of him. He had also been relied upon to protect his village and, in this regard, he had failed. The opinions the villagers had of him didn't overly worry Mecedah. He knew people only reacted to what they saw and his actions so far had appeared to be disappointing.

The Spaniards were pleased that the old chief had been discredited. He lived alone and camped at the cave in the vicinity of the mine. There was apparently no need to be concerned about this old man who seemed destined to waste the rest of his life by hunting and sitting beside his fire in front of the cave.

Being underestimated actually helped the old man. No one bothered him, or his scattered villagers, when a soldier vanished. One at a time, and sometimes in small groups, soldiers failed to reach, or return from, the mine. Such occurrences had been taking place since the attack on the village and the forced labor of many villagers in the mine.

Mecedah's most frequent visitor was a coyote. This coyote was friendly only with Mecedah and seemed to be as much an outcast from the world of wolves as Mecedah was from the society of people. Mecedah called his friend Cat Hunter, or Cat, because this wolf hated mountain lions and would growl when he detected their scents. Possibly a mountain lion had killed the other members of Cat's family.

"I suppose everyone thinks we're sort o' useless," said Mecedah to the animal while the two companions rested beside the fire in front of the cave. The wolf always seemed to be smiling about something or, at least, amused by his lot in life. The old man's words were comforting sounds. Cat understood the meanings of some of these sounds. "Actually though, you're a great help to me," said Mecedah. "You give me company and you are never here when other people are around. Therefore, if you are with me, I can relax. If you are away, I have to be alert and careful. You don't like cats or people. Maybe soldiers killed the rest o' your family-like my family was killed. You're with me now, so I

5

know there are no other people around. I should call you Signal in addition to Cat."

Mecedah added a few sticks of dry aspen to his smokeless fire. Next, he shared a chunk of smoked elk with Cat. Both wolf and man chewed contentedly while watching the patch of the river they could see from the camp.

Cat had acquired the habit of chewing food-or, at least, eating it in small pieces-because in Mecedah's camp there was enough to eat and a wolf didn't have to gulp food to be sure of getting it before something else took it. Mecedah watched a moose wading in the river. This day, Mecedah didn't have to go hunting to get more food and he considered most animals to be his friends. The river was a particularly important friend. The man and river were much alike.

They both appeared to be calm on the surface yet brimmed with life.

I linger on this earth to finish my work before I re—enter the spirit world, reflected Mecedah. The Spaniards attacked our village, killing many people, including men, women and children. Our villagers are being used to work in the mine. These workers die and are replaced. If this work continues, we will all die and the Spaniards will have to get slaves from other villages. I have heard that these cruel enemies have killed many people in other places. The soldiers want everything we have-our towns, our people, our land and its gold. We use gold for decorations. The enemies want this gold more than any other thing. Our people don't respect me because they think I haven't done anything to protect them. Actually I only seem to be doing nothing while I am always working either with plans or actions. I have destroyed many of these enemies and hidden their weapons. Some men of my village have agreed to follow me when I call on them to drive out the soldiers who are killing us. The river has always been my friend and it will help me. I've waited many years. I sit here like the trees around me. Many seasons have whistled across my branches, bringing me to this time when I must complete my work. Afterward, I will leave my cherished piece of land and rejoin the spirit world. My bones will nourish the trees as the forest has nourished me.

Cat stood up nervously. He looked eastward, then walked in the opposite direction, moving out of view beyond adjacent pines. Shortly afterward, a man, known as Blue Raven, entered the camp and sat down beside the fire. He received smoked elk from Mecedah.

The two men appeared, in some respects, to be opposites. Mecedah was an older man with gray hair and a lined face. However, muscles rippled on his lean body. For an old man who apparently didn't do anything, he was strong. Strength was mainly revealed in his eyes. They possessed a sparkling fire.

In regard to strength, the two men were similar, although Blue Raven was younger and had a prominent nose shaped like an eagle's beak. The men reminded each other of an eagle, particularly the bird's spirit.

"What have you been seeing?" asked Blue Raven.

"In a vision, I saw soldiers upside down in the river," replied

Mecedah. "The river is our friend and will help us to get rid of these enemies. We must remove them before they kill all of us. What have you been seeing?"

"I have been watching the mine," answered Blue Raven. "There is the same, large group of soldiers camped near this mine. About the same number of soldiers are coming from the south. They are bringing more workers for the mine to replace our people who have died."

"I have waited for the right time and this chance is with us now," said Mecedah. "I feel and see the presence of a great opportunity. Gather the other men with the weapons we have saved. Those of us who like the river will wait in the water. Our other men can conceal themselves in the forest. We will kill the approaching enemies and take their weapons. Afterward, we must attack the soldiers at the mine. From this time onward, we have to be more watchful like the hawk or eagle. We must not give our enemies a chance again to hurt us."

"This is the decision I've been waiting for," exclaimed Blue Raven with his face glowing. "I can't wait any longer-or rest. I'll get our people ready for the river and the mine."

"Have our men watch both groups of enemies and I'll meet you at the river where the soldiers always cross," said Mecedah.

Watching the younger man leaving the camp, Mecedah felt relieved and confident. The day he had waited for, through many seasons, had come. Everything was in place. He had done all the work and made every plan. Having prepared everything, he could now relax and watch his plans unfold. Like the pines around him, he had watched many winter snows whistle passed him. These winters had brought a time that was right for him to carry out his work. Later, he could rest until he rejoined the spirit world.

On the morning of the battle, in the year of 1778, the soldiers were clearly not expecting trouble. The first rider nudged his horse into the greenish blue water. Other riders and horses followed. Captives were in the center of the column. More soldiers bunched their horses together at the back of the line.

The river quickly deepened, sending cold water swirling around the riders. Horses surged ahead. Water splashed amid struggling animals and men. In such confusion, more men came out of the foaming water. Clubs flashed through the mist and spray, knocking soldiers under churning water. Panicked horses bolted and sent more screaming riders plunging into the blood stained river. Mecedah's men fought furiously, releasing rage that had been festering for years.

The battle had been lost before the soldiers realized they were in one. When all the soldiers drifted in the river, Mecedah's men freed captives and collected weapons.

The soldiers' camp in front of the mine was generally quiet except for the clanging sounds of cooking equipment being used and a murmur of voices as men talked while preparing a morning meal. Guns were stacked away from small fires that provided heat for the preparation of food and coffee. The dawn seemed sleepy and uneventful like the others had been.

Aspens added patches of gold to a predominantly green background of ponderosa pines. Magpies chattered at the edge of camp. Resonant croaking calls of ravens rang through the mist before an eerie silence stalked the area. A sense of normalcy seemed to resume when a muted whispering of voices started again added to an occasional clang of some cooking equipment being dropped or tapped.

Mecedah's men, bolting from the woods, caught the camp so completely off guard that the runners initially had little, or no, opposition. Rushing men came like a gust of wind hurling amid the cooking fires. Some soldiers were clubbed before they knew what had caused the sudden commotion. Tents toppling into fires sent a pall of smoke billowing across an open area where men started fighting in small skirmishes amid popping sounds of gunshots. The raiders all ran in one direction, returning to the forest and vanishing from view almost as suddenly as they had appeared. Gathering in an haughty rage, the soldiers pursued these men who had struck with such speed and deadliness.

Just as the soldiers entered the forest, they were hit again by waiting attackers. Helmets and breastplates provided little protection when, at close range, arrows, clubs or bullets struck at shocked faces. Soldiers, who could still walk, struggled back to the protection of their camp where they tried to form a defensive circle. Burning tents provided dark, acrid smoke that obscured frantic defensive efforts. Bodies burning in fires added an ominous stench to the camp while everything that could be moved was used to form an encircling barricade.

Mecedah wouldn't risk the extra injuries to his men that might come from a direct assault on the barricade. Through years of waiting for the right time to strike, Mecedah had learned to be patient. He had become far too patient to get hasty now that he had his enemies trapped. He gave the signal for arrows to be shot skyward to rain down on the sprawled and waiting soldiers.

An eerie silence gripped the area as drifting smoke concealed the movements of workers leaving the mine. Wedges of sunlight shot through breaks in foliage and between trunks while the sun slowly crossed the sky before descending into a crimson haze along the western horizon. This glow gradually lost its brightness and faded until becoming lost in a pale sheen from a silver moon. An owl hooted then there were only occasional cries of soldiers hit by a relentless, bitter sprinkle of arrows.

"Our enemies must know they will all die if they stay behind their barricade," Mecedah said to Blue Raven. "They have to try to escape along the trail to the river. Position our people beside the trail and also in the river. None of these soldiers will escape. If others come back this way again, they will not get passed the river."

"The people will wait for these enemies," replied Blue Raven before he moved away through the shadows.

The night drifted away like tendrils of mist curling through

17

moonlight. An owl hooted four times and Mecedah answered with a similar, hooting call. The people were ready. But the enemies were also patient. They could sense death and did not want to rush its approach any further.

Among the defenders inside the barricade, there was one soldier, Ortega Cortez, who was not like the others. His heart had knotted when he saw the massacres of the villagers. He did not like to have people forced to work at the mine. Cruelty always left a cold feeling in his soul and he felt chilled often. He was the best cook in the camp and he was now the only one alive who knew much about medicine. He did the best he could for the dying men. He advised them to leave the arrowheads in the wounds because removing the points caused too much loss of blood. A real doctor could later remove them. The shafts were cut away, leaving the points for another time if there was to be more time.

I always fed the birds at the edge of camp, thought Ortega after sipping coffee. I have fed the slaves as well as the soldiers. I provided a little kindness in a sea of cruelty. I'm haunted by the killings I've seen. The soldiers talk about other massacres. I read the reports. The senseless killing troubles me. Killing in battle is one thing. Unnecessary battles present another situation entirely and the continuing massacre of villagers after a battle is unforgivable. The people we have attacked are now attacking us. I understand my attackers better than the soldiers with whom I will die.

Each person has to face his or her accounting with God and, at least, I will not be ashamed when my time comes. I've done my best and therefore I'm content. I don't fear dying. It will be for me, maybe, a relief. If I had been in charge, I would have treated people equally and let these villagers be as they themselves chose to be. Let each village live and we can trade with each other.

Ortega finished drinking the coffee. He had a disquieting feeling of impending trouble. Soldiers were stirring, preparing to abandon their fortification.

When a bank of clouds covered the moon, there was a rush to escape from the barricade. The uninjured soldiers ran first followed by a line of stragglers. This stream of escaping forms was met by sporadic blasts of shots. Arrows whizzed from the shadows and men screamed. Flashing clubs shortened many screams. Two soldiers reached the river. Soon after they entered the water, their blood flowed ahead of their bodies, drifting downstream. When the cook made his way across the river and reached the opposite bank, no weapon was turned against him.

Ortega walked southward until he came to the army headquarters. He reported the presence of so many enemies to the north that the army moved south, abandoning the northern mountains.

Ortega's home prospered and he became a wealthy rancher. He rode north twice to the mountains that would later be called the Uintas. Each time, he visited Mecedah. The two men talked about how things could have been without the ruthless killings. The men discussed their dreams and, in their spirits, they walked among the mountains.

TWO

GRAY HAWK

When Mecedah's nephew, Gray Hawk, was a young man, the Blackfoot attacked his village. The leader of this Shoshoni village was Cameahwait and, in 1805, they were camped beside the Lemhi River in the Beaverhead Mountains, northwest of the Uintas.

Gray Hawk had been sleeping with his wife, Otter, in their teepee when the hide structure was torn from its base in an explosion of tumbling poles, possessions and hide coverings. Reacting instantly with empowering fury, he sprang at the closest rider, knocking him from his horse. The man grabbed for Gray Hawk's eyes while Gray Hawk pulled a tomahawk from this attacker's belt and sank the weapon into his forehead.

Seeing Otter running for cover beyond plunging horses, Gray Hawk withdrew the tomahawk then mounted an horse that had become entangled by the teepee's poles and covering. Gray Hawk pulled a spear from the ground. He was about to ride in the direction his wife had taken when a Blackfoot man left his horse and was leaping at Gray Hawk. While in the air, this man met the spear's point. It pierced the large, attacker's body before the form, in a spray of blood, hit Gray Hawk's horse and slid to the ground. From this man, Gray Hawk took a second tomahawk. He was putting the weapon inside his belt as he was struck on the side of his head. Dazed, he hung on to his horse and nudged it toward the route that Otter had taken.

Gray Hawk regained consciousness in the woods. His head throbbed with pain. There was a gash in his side. He welcomed sleep as it returned. He rested in the woods until he felt well enough to ride. He returned to the village and checked the losses. Men had been killed. Some people were missing, including Otter.

Gray Hawk was a tall man. His lean, well-muscled body had numerous old, as well as the recent, scars, although he only fought when necessary. He preferred to live a quiet life hunting and fishing. Mainly, he considered himself to be a fisherman and he enjoyed living in the mountains. He often visited Mecedah and sat beside the camp fire, listening to Mecedah tell stories about the mountains and river.

Gray Hawk could not concentrate on anything except finding his missing wife. He rode northward to the hot spring. He drank this water and relaxed in its warmth. Feeling rejuvenated, he resumed traveling along the trail of his enemies.

The trail led north to the site of a buffalo hunt. Hunters had shot many animals. Women were busy saving hides and food. With such a quantity of meat, there was much work to do. Gray Hawk recognized two women from his village. He did not see his wife.

I'll talk to those women, Gray Hawk said to himself. They'll know about Otter. Everyone is busy. They're distracted by a successful hunt. They will not be expecting, or watching for, one enemy.

One of the Shoshoni women was working at a buffalo that had fallen away from most of the others. I've had an empty feeling since my wife was taken, observed Gray Hawk. Finding her, will involve risk to my life, yet my life feels less important-smaller-without her. Getting her back at any time is risky. Acting now is maybe less risky than during some other occasion when my enemies are expecting trouble.

Gray Hawk had deliberately covered himself with dust for camouflage. He had also been lying on clayish and sandy ground. His horse was tethered behind him to one of a large number of cottonwood trees. The morning was warm. A gentle breeze stirred grass. Blackfoot horses grazed while people talked and worked.

Gray Hawk proceeded cautiously toward an horse containing a Spanish saddle. Reigns dragged while the animal fed. It did not shy away when Gray Hawk took the reigns. He led the animal to the shoshoni woman.

Gray Hawk asked the woman about his wife. The woman said Otter had been badly injured resisting capture and had died at another camping place.

Using signs, Gray Hawk asked the second Shoshoni woman, who was working nearby, to get an horse and ride it to the cottonwoods. Upon receiving these instructions, the woman started walking. An old woman shouted at her; but the Shoshoni used signs to reply and the old woman went back to her work.

The Shoshoni woman tied a long piece of rope to an horse's dangling reigns. As she walked toward the cottonwoods, the animal, nudged by the rope, appeared to be willfully following her.

Gray Hawk helped the other Shoshoni woman carry a buffalo hide containing chunks of meat. The two people carried this burden and the horse followed, being tied by a buffalo hide thong.

If we rode the horses, we would be too noticeable, thought Gray Hawk. When we are carrying meat, we appear to be working like the others.

Gray Hawk and the two women reached the trees and mounted the horses. Rushing southward, each rider felt the full excitement and relief of escaping. Letting the women go first, Gray Hawk rode last to protect them. Inside his belt, he had a tomahawk and a knife. He also kept his bow and arrows ready for trouble.

Trouble came quickly. Hearing the pounding of hooves behind him, he turned and saw three horsemen. Two were approaching from the cottonwoods while another raced from the west. Gray Hawk kept riding southward. The women were well ahead of him.

The three pursuers closed to form one cloud of dust behind Gray Hawk. In front of him, one of the women's horses fell. The rider remounted with the other woman then they continued moving southward.

The fallen horse tried to stand on three legs. After tumbling once, the animal stood shakily while one leg dangled uselessly.

This might be the mistake of a lifetime, thought Gray Hawk before he dismounted and slapped his horse with the bow, sending the animal racing after the women. The

Blackfoot horsemen were approaching rapidly adding more dust to an haze kicked up by the first horses. When the pursuers saw the crippled horse, they knew this was a first sign of victory. These men urged their mounts on to greater speed. An arrow, coming from behind the crippled horse stuck in the side of the closest man. He plunged from his horse as the other men turned and charged toward the crippled animal.

Another arrow sank into the face of a second man, sending him flailing backwards over his galloping horse. The third rider sprang from his mount and slammed into Gray Hawk, knocking him to the ground. Grabbing the man's throat, Gray Hawk pulled out his knife and shoved it upward as he was hit on the head.

Gray Hawk regained consciousness with pain searing through his head. Although a tomahawk had hit him, the blow had been lessened by the knife's thrust. He pulled his knife from the dead man. He slew the crippled horse. After collecting the other mounts, he rode south, following the tracks left by the women's horse.

There was celebrating in the camp when the women arrived followed later by Gray Hawk. He continued to have an empty feeling because of the loss of his wife. He had an increasing interest, though, in one of the women he had rescued from the Blackfoot camp. Her name was White Shell and her husband had been killed during the attack.

With White Shell's company, Gray Hawk's spirit revived. He often went to the fishing place at the Lochsa, or Kooskooskee, River. He watched the cold, murmuring water while he rested and fished. He often thought about his uncle, Mecedah, and his friend, Old Toby. These two men had accomplished more during their older years than in their younger days. Gray Hawk saw his own life unfolding in the opposite way. He had accomplished much early in his life. Now there seemed to be little for him to do. Maybe he would marry White Shell then move to the mountains where Mecedah had lived. Mecedah fished in the river and camped near the mine worked by the Spaniards. That mine had been abandoned. Gray Hawk was pleased with the piece of yellow stone he had received in trade from the mine farther to the south.

Holding his amulet of yellow stone fastened to a leather cord around his neck, Gray Hawk said to himself, I must trade for more yellow stone from the southern mine. I'll get some for White Shell. Like myself, Mecedah preferred the southern stone. My friend, Old Toby, knows about such places. He is now working for the Americans and will show them the trails through these mountains.

Gray Hawk was resting at the fishing place on the Lochsa River when Old Toby arrived. He was with the Americans. They turned away from the river and started climbing the mountainside, heading toward the upper trail. They stopped at the spring.

Gray Hawk gave the hungry travelers smoked fish and berries. He was served a drink that the red haired chief, William Clark, called Hyson tea. Gray Hawk enjoyed meeting these people. They helped to restore

34

his spirit. He noticed that the red haired chief was strong and respected by the Americans as well as the Shoshonis. They all talked to each other by signs and different languages. Chief Cameahwait's sister, Sacagawea, known as Bird Woman, was guiding the Americans. She was an attractive looking woman. She spoke to her husband, Charbonneau, using the Minitari language. He talked to Labiche in French. This man spoke English to Clark. Gray Hawk got his information from Sacagawea and Old Toby.

When Sacagawea introduced Gray Hawk to Clark, the red haired chief asked Gray Hawk about the trail to the west. Gray Hawk said he had mainly traveled south to visit his uncle, Mecedah who lived in the mountains. Clark was very interested when Gray Hawk told him about the

Spaniards who wore helmets and breastplates. Gray Hawk also described the abandoned mine. Gray Hawk thought he was much like Clark. They were both strong as well as tall.

By way of the translators, Gray Hawk said to Clark, "If other Americans are like you, we can trade with you. In our village now, there are only three guns. We need more guns to protect ourselves from our enemies. They are getting guns from traders in the north and east."

"We will give you guns in trade," said Clark. "We want to bring you trade and peace." While these words were being translated, Clark gave Gray Hawk a Peace and Friendship Medal, showing the American President, Jefferson, on one side and clasped hands along with a trade tomahawk and pipe on the other. In return, Gray Hawk gave Clark the yellow stone. Clark knew it to be iron pyrite.

"Where does the yellow stone come from?" asked Clark.

"Far to the south," replied Gray Hawk.

Gray Hawk's spirit revived during this meeting with the strong, honest and sincere leader, William Clark. Gray Hawk looked forward to trading with the Americans. He knew that if more guns could be acquired through trade, the Shoshonis could protect their land against all enemies. He had enjoyed this meeting and was intrigued by the people in the camp. They were weary and short of food. Gray Hawk shared his smoked fish and berries. He liked Clark's tea and was pleased when Sacagawea poured more.

While Gray Hawk respected Clark, he detested Charbonneau. Charbonneau was a dirty, sloppy man. Gray Hawk thought this man was a scavenger in life. The Minitaris had been the first to capture Sacagawea then she was captured by Charbonneau. Clark used Charbonneau, Francois Labiche and Sacagawea for translating. Gray Hawk could see that Sacagawea looked at Clark as her real husband. Life happens strangely sometimes, thought Gray Hawk. Clark and I could be friends although our words have to be translated. Sacagawea is trapped by one man and sees another as her husband. From these people, I have received a new interest in life. I will take White Shell to Mecedah's mountains.

THREE

ARON KELLAR

Aron Kellar was born in 1840, the year the beaver supply dwindled to almost nothing in the Uinta Mountains along with surrounding area. He was raised in a cabin, near the mine in the Uintas, until his parents died from a fever caused largely by hard times and worries. Looking for an easier life, Aron headed north, becoming an hide hunter, shooting mainly wolves and buffalo.

By the spring of 1873, Aron had been through an hard life. His reddish brown hair was receding. He was of average height, although he was unusually strong and could work most of a day without tiring. His eyes were brown and he had sufficiently good eyesight to be a better than average marksman.

Aron considered the collection of hides to be a necessary way of making money; yet he never did get to like the killing. Other hide hunters and wolfers enjoyed killing or thought little about it. Many hunters found the shooting to be exciting. Aron was also different from some other trappers in his desire to keep himself as clean as possible. However, the main characteristic, separating him from the men with whom he worked, was the chill he felt when he saw a person get killed. He felt sorry for the animals he killed and he respected them. He disliked most of the hide hunters and had no toleration for the harming of people.

On or about the first day of May, in 1873, Aron Kellar was in Abel Farwell's trading post. Aron found himself in the midst of trouble that was stirring with the other trappers. Horses had been stolen from a group of fifteen trappers and traders in Montana. Tracks of horses went north to the Cypress Hills in Canada. The men, led by Thomas Hardwick and John Evans, camped beside Battle Creek, south of Abel Farwell's trading post. North of this post, there was an Assiniboine village of about forty lodges led by Little Chief. The Assiniboines had come down from the north. They were in a weakened condition because of a shortage of food during the previous winter.

Three more trappers and traders, who had also lost horses, joined the other fifteen men. Aron Kellar had the coldest feeling he had ever experienced as he walked with Abel Farwell and approached the traders. Aron looked on hopelessly as Abel tried to reason with the eighteen men who had positioned themselves in a coulee beside the Assiniboine village. The traders had Henry repeating rifles.

Aron Kellar felt the chill that day when the men started firing at the people in the village. Few escaped. They ran to the hills.

Aron's world turned upside down during this shooting, remembered as the Cypress Hills Massacre. He didn't know that this massacre showed politicians in Ottawa the need for a western, police force and, consequently, Prime Minister, Sir John A. Macdonald, established the North West Mounted Police.

Aron Kellar abandoned the company and work of trappers. He started traveling with two other men who were robbing settlers crossing the Oregon Trail.

FOUR

THE OUTLAWS

Aron Kellar started his outlaw days after he met Oliver Kimble and Mat Chivington. Both Oliver and Mat had drifted into becoming outlaws because of laziness. They didn't want to work at anything other than taking money from settlers. Oliver was a large man who was slow at everything including thinking. He had black hair and a moustache. His eyes were dark and glossy. He dressed sloppily maybe because his size worked against neatness. Mat had similarly dark hair and eyes in addition to a beard. He was slim and as shifty as a weasel. Aron rode with these two men for little further reason other than he met them on the trail.

Aron did the scouting because he was skilled at reading tracks. He was an adequate cook and was kind to the horses. Aron was thereby useful for looking after the group while Oliver and Mat robbed travelers, mainly settlers. Thefts were limited particularly to money and jewelry because large items could not be easily transported and cached.

Aron, Oliver and Mat always seemed to be short of food. They were hungry and tracking buffalo when they heard shots ahead. The men proceeded onward cautiously.

Upon coming to the top of an hill, they saw a group of settlers who had shot a buffalo and were starting to butcher it. They had three wagons. Likely these people were part of a larger group and had stopped to get fresh meat. There were children, women and four men. Each man reached for a gun when the three riders approached.

Oliver and Mat were not brave men. They seemed reckless sometimes because they rarely did much thinking before acting. Aron was always cautious. While working with Oliver and Mat, Aron knew he was not dealing with friends. The settlers also looked hostile. They were ready for trouble.

Approaching closely enough to be heard, Oliver said, "We were trailin' this buffalo. You are welcome to a share."

"That's our meat," stated one settler. "We have families to look after. There were other animals. You can keep trailin' them." This man, doing the talking, was a crusty person. An eagle feather was attached to the side of a weathered and stained hat. Badly torn trousers were kept in place by suspenders. The man's face mainly appeared to be hairy because long strands extended below the hat and he also had a bristling beard.

"A share o' this is all we need," replied Oliver with fake friendliness. "We have other things to trade."

"We have families to look after," stated the hairy man unwaveringly. "We're not takin' any chances with strangers. You move on. There's other meat around."

Oliver was cornered and sweating. His wits searched feebly for a way out of a corner his own carelessness had put himself into again. Deciding to stall, he asked, "Could we do some tradin'? We'd like to get coffee."

A boy and a girl brought horses to the men beside the buffalo. The settler who had done the talking mounted one horse while another man mounted the second animal. The two other settlers took firing positions behind the buffalo. The mounted settlers rode toward the outlaws. The talkative man approached Oliver who had ridden out in front of Mat and Aron.

Oliver stretched out his right hand in greeting. Surprisingly and foolishly, the hairy man accepted the greeting. His social training in courtesy was a weakness in dealing with a scavenger like Oliver. While shaking the Plainsman's right hand, Oliver grasped a pistol with his left hand and shot the man in the chest. The man tumbled backwards off his horse. With one foot caught in the stirrup, the dead man was dragged away by the bolting horse. The other mounted settler shot Oliver in the face, sending his second, pistol blast screaming over the person's head. A well placed shot, from a settler behind the buffalo, buckled Mat and he dropped off his horse. Another shot scraped Arlo's arm. He wheeled his horse around and rode back the way he had come. Bullets searched for him until he reached the far side of the hill.

When he was certain he wasn't being pursued, he rode slowly, letting his horse rest. Returning to the regular camping place, Arlo got the stolen jewelry along with money that Oliver and Mat had stashed. Arlo took this loot to the abandoned mine in the Uinta Mountains.

The mine had been used as a resting-place and hideout for Oliver and Mat. They had picked up the local stories about the site. Aron had always considered this area to be his home. He knew the mine had been operated by Spaniards who had forced the Indians to do the work until they successfully revolted. Retreating Spaniards had left behind helmets and breastplates. There was also a medallion on an upper ledge. This medal had President Jefferson's name and picture on one surface. On the other side, there were clasped hands along with a crossed pipe and tomahawk. Not wanting to interfere with the medal, or its owner, Aron left it on the ledge. He remembered when he was a boy living in a cabin near the mine. His parents trapped and traded. Brigham Young and the Mormons had worked the mine about the same time, around the year of 1850. The Mormons had left the mine when it stopped producing gold.

Young might have thought the mine was starting to yield only iron pyrite because the Indians had iron pyrite and used this stone for decorations. Actually the iron pyrite came from the mine north of Canyon De Chelly in Arizona.

Aron Kellar found the Indian system of trading to be elaborate and fascinating. He started a trading post near the Uinta mine. He carried on a steady trading business with the Shoshonis and Utes.

The Indians accepted Aron because he treated each customer fairly. The Shoshonis respected Aron as they had respected Jim Bridger. Like Bridger, Aron traded guns to the Shoshonis. Earlier in their history, the Shoshonis had suffered because their enemies possessed more guns. After obtaining a sufficient number of guns from traders like Jim Bridger and Aron Kellar, the Shoshonis became very powerful and fully able to protect their land from enemies.

Aron Kellar, for a short time, worked in a mine at Deadwood in the Black Hills. While he was in Deadwood, he visited a saloon where he met Catrina, or Cat, Newman. Aron could not get over the fact she was a saloon girl just as he couldn't recover from the effect of meeting her. He was with her when Wild Bill Hickok was killed during a poker game in 1876.

Aron was almost killed in the saloon. He was sitting beside a table and drinking whisky with Catrina. She had dark, brown eyes and auburn hair. She was about five feet tall and slim. Cat kept her hair so clean it shone. Her dark eyes sparkled as she talked with Aron. She was accepting his proposal to leave town and go to his trading post when a tall, burly, bearded miner hauled her up to a standing position. She was pulled so forcefully that the table was knocked over, spilling the drinks. With an arm gripping her firmly around the waist, he said, "Come on. I need some company over at my table."

Fury ignited in Aron. He sprang forward, clamping his arms around the departing man's neck. Aron was dragged, amid tumbling tables and scrambling customers, to the miner's table next to the bar. Here the large man turned to face Aron then shoved him away as if he was more of a nuisance than a threat. Aron raged back with fists flying until a powerful hand grabbed his throat. The fingers started to squeeze until Aron could no longer breath. He sensed his eyes bulging and felt his life was ending just before he drew his pistol and fired three muffled shots into the giant's chest. The fingers loosened their iron grip. The man stared blankly at blood spewing from holes in his shirt as he sank to the floor.

Keeping his gun pointed at faces around the room, Aron followed Cat to the doorway. They stepped outside and ran to get their horses. Riding out of town, Aron and Cat took indirect routes that eventually led to the trading post in the Uintas.

Cat found her first, real home in the Uintas. She enjoyed helping Aron run the trading post. They had one son, named Tyrell, born in 1877. The trading post, the mine and the Uinta Mountains all became Tyrell's home.

Following the death of his parents, taken by smallpox, Tyrell headed to the south. He felt he had to get away after the loss of his parents. Having heard about the iron pyrite mine, north of Canyon De Chelly, Tyrell thought this might be a good place to look for gold and start a new life. Before he left the Uinta mine, he hid the Kellar jewelry by using jewels as temper. They were mixed with clay to make large, pottery bowls. The bowls, containing the unusual grit, or stones, were too large to take away so he thought the Kellar fortune would remain at the abandoned mine in the Uintas.

FIVE

TYRELL KELLAR

Tyrell Kellar took a supply of gold with him when he left the Uintas. He traveled to Canyon De Chelly in Arizona. Next he drove north and, with the help of the Navajos, he located the iron pyrite mine. The Indians had used this material for decorations. Tyrell thought this natural landmark would be a good location for a trading post. He also expanded the mine in an effort to locate gold.

He soon abandoned the trading post idea because the site was too isolated. He concentrated his efforts on working the mine although he didn't really need money because he had a sufficient supply of gold from the Uintas.

Since Tyrell already had gold before he started mining, he put little effort into the work. He was a tall, lean person who kept his long, brown hair tied at the back of his head with a leather cord. His eyes were black and he neatly trimmed a grayish red moustache.

He became a lazy man who got his pleasures in life just by living with an awareness of the beauty and interest provided by each day. He put less effort into making or building things. He traveled only far enough and often enough to locate a wife. He brought her back to live at his house beside the mine. Her name was Yolanda Perkins. She was a large, strong person with blond hair and blue eyes.

Being accustomed to hard work, Yolanda looked after her home, giving Tyrell more time to observe life. Yolanda and Tyrell had one daughter and a son. The daughter, Catherine, was born in 1919 while the son, Cliff, was born in 1920.

The gold that Tyrell brought from the Uinta mine caused his laziness and also his death. When he used gold in order to purchase supplies, people started to say this gold came from the mine he was working near his house.

Tyrell enjoyed living in the desert. He had a particular fondness for the beauty of cacti although he could never develop a tolerance for rattlesnakes. His favorite animal was the coyote. Tyrell didn't hunt for meat because he could buy all his supplies.

Life seemed to be going well for Tyrell. When his son, Cliff, became old enough to work, he took over the mining. Tyrell's daughter, Catherine, was able to do any of the homestead's chores and she could do them as well as her mother.

The five bandits who attacked the Tyrell mine were hardened men and they desperately needed money. They attacked at daybreak as the first rays of sunlight were emblazoning the tops of distant mesas and rock spires.

The initial volley of shots blasted through the house's windows, killing Yolanda and Catherine in the kitchen. The shooting awakened Tyrell who was in his bed. Cliff dropped his pickaxe in the mine. He checked his rifle, making sure it was loaded.

Tyrell, pointing his rifle out the shattered bedroom window, shot a bullet into the surprised face of an hulking bandit who toppled over backwards. After dropping a second attacker with another shot, Tyrell slumped to the floor. A bullet had torn into his chest.

From the mine's entrance, Cliff shot a bandit just as he was starting to point his rifle toward the mine. This man fired at the ground then fell on his rifle. He had been guarding five tethered horses.

Two outlaws approached the horses. One man put his boot in a stirrup and was swinging up onto the saddle when Cliff's bullet knocked him back to the ground. The other man scrambled out of view.

Cliff did not like the feeling of not knowing where his enemies had gone. He remained motionless while he watched the terrain and house. Clumps of prickly pear cactus offered concealment for raiders. The horses remained beside the cottonwoods. Beyond these trees, there were mesquite trees and creosote bushes.

An unnatural silence hung ominously over the area like the stench of gun smoke or death. Cliff's mind teemed with worries. The house was too quiet. Maybe, like himself, the other members of his family were waiting silently. A clammy chill of fear gradually seeped through him until it dried his mouth. Fear seemed to have a metallic taste. His heart beat more rapidly. The morning, although sunlit, contained a cold, gray haze. Such grayness came more from his feelings rather than from anything lurking outside around his home. My fear tells me I'm the only one left alive along with one enemy, thought Cliff. The land is too quiet and so is the house. There isn't anything stirring anywhere.

Gripped by a feeling of dread, Cliff recalled a series of memories. They flashed through his mind as he reviewed his life at the mine. He had enjoyed his home with his hardworking mother and sister. His father, although somewhat lazy, was a constant and loyal friend who enjoyed talking. He was a trusted confidant. He had been given a deed to property, including a mine, in the Uintas. In this mine, jewelry had been stashed in pottery jugs.

Without entirely knowing about the loss of his family, Cliff could feel the emptiness. Vultures circled through a pale sky while Cliff waited and watched for a sound or sign of his enemies. These outlaws had come to kill in order to get gold. Cliff was sure only one man remained of the five who had attacked. Five horses had been tied to cottonwoods. Maybe the one remaining man would reveal himself when he tried to get his horse.

Struck by an overwhelming rush of panic, Cliff felt he had to check his family. He darted toward the horses, drawing a shot from somewhere to his side. The bullet whizzed passed his face. He turned toward this blast and, as he walked forward, he fired at the tops of rocks. He stopped shooting, keeping the gun ready, while he hastened toward the source of the shot.

Hearing a scratching sound of cactus scraping against cloth or leather, he turned just before the form of a man sprang at him and forced him to stumble backwards into a tangle of prickly pear cactus. Numerous barbs jabbed him, searing his body with pain. He rebounded quickly to a standing position. Swinging his rifle like a club, he knocked a knife from the attacker's hand. Screaming, this man held his hand while Cliff grasped the knife. He turned the weapon toward his enemy then shot the blade upward.

The outlaw removed the crimson knife. He attempted to thrust the blade forward; but the expression on his face turned blank and he slumped to the ground.

Cliff Kellar restored his life gradually. He reassembled pieces slowly, adding parts occasionally. During the following years, he added a partner to help work the mine. The

partner's name was Zackery Tomkins
and his wife was Rita.

SIX

ZACKERY TOMKINS

The arrangement, of having the partners, Cliff and Zack, work the mine while Zack's wife, Rita, looked after the house, was, at first, a sensible way to make a comfortable home in the desert region of northeastern Arizona. Cliff enjoyed having company while he poked around at the mine. He was a tall, strong man with blue eyes and brown hair. His face had been lined and tanned by the sun. He wore glasses and liked to work with tools. He didn't talk about his inherited stash of gold from the mine in the Uintas. Hidden, with the gold, he kept a deed to the Uinta property. He intended to go back to the Uinta mine because his father had told him about precious stones, such as diamonds, hidden in pottery jugs cached at the mine.

Zack was a flat-faced man with brown hair and eyes. He was seriously overweight and preferred to not do any strenuous work. He didn't want to actually work at the mine. He liked prospecting. He spent more and more of his time, out on the arid land, looking for traces of gold.

Zackery thought he had hit the discovery of a lifetime when he located a site that must have been worked by the Spaniards about an hundred years in the past. A stone basin had been built to hold water seeping from the base of a rock wall. Close to this spring, a shelter had been constructed of stones. A crude furnace was also formed with rocks. The furnace had been used as a smelter to refine ore. The Spaniards had to build a crude smelter because, when they returned to the south, they could carry with them only the pure gold. Close to this smelter, there was an entranceway to a roughly cut mine. Weathered beams had broken allowing much of the ceiling to collapse, leaving little more than a small cave on the side of an hill.

Zack, for the first time in his life, felt a surge of greed. This mine was his. He intended to restrict all his prospecting to checking the mine. It had produced gold at one time and likely would again. Maybe the refined gold never left the mine. Gold bars could've been stored inside before the tunnel collapsed. Apaches might have killed or driven away the miners before they could deplete the mine or take away the gold bars.

Zackery lived in his truck while he worked at the mine. Slowly, he removed clayish earth and rocks from the caved in tunnel. He replaced the broken beams with new, cottonwood logs. He disliked such hard, sweaty work; however, he was pushed onward by a fever of greed mixed with a desire for wealth and its promise of an easier life.

In addition to chipping away at debris in the mine, Zack rested by doing some prospecting in the surrounding area and picked up a few nuggets from an adjacent ridge. He used this gold to buy supplies for the work at his new mine.

He was using a pickaxe to dislodge rocks and clayish earth from the base of the tunnel when he uncovered bones mixed with fragments of cloth and leather. Imbedded in one, of two, human skulls, there was a flint arrowhead. Zack's hands trembled while he nudged the arrowhead lodged in the skull. If the Spaniards were all killed by Apaches, he said to himself, the gold bars will be at the back of this tunnel-unless the Apaches removed them. If some of the miners survived, they might have hidden part of the gold then escaped with as much loot as they could carry. Cliff should help me work here rather than waste his time in an iron pyrite mine.

While Zackery was living in his truck and working at his new mine, Cliff was back at the house doing some prospecting of his own. He was prospecting Rita's mind, finding her to be increasingly both interesting and baffling. The main nugget he found was companionship. Rita was an attractive woman. She had blondish-brown hair and blue eyes. She remained slim and strong because she was always working at cooking in addition to doing other homestead chores. Her tea biscuits, topped by butter and honey, were the best that Cliff had ever tasted.

After Zack had been absent for a stretch of eight weeks, Rita decided she would trade a companion she didn't have for one she did have. She persuaded Cliff to leave with her and take her to his home beside the mine in the Uinta Mountains.

SIX

FESTON TUCKER

Feston Tucker was a free lance writer. He sent articles anywhere although he preferred the newspapers in San Francisco. He considered San Francisco to be the newspaper capitol of the world. He also enjoyed the city's comparatively safe, clean, businesslike atmosphere with a climate that wasn't too hot or cold. He just liked this city and its beauty, particularly during crisp mornings when mist obscured the Golden Gate Bridge, leaving only a faint outline. Alcatraz Island added picturesque history to the scenery surrounding this bustling city where Feston enjoyed working.

Feston Tucker was a little less than six feet tall. His graying hair was kept somewhat long. He had dark brown eyes and swarthy features. He was strong because he did much physical work to track down stories. Often, he got inside his stories and was occasionally injured while pursuing information. Since he learned about life the hard way, his stories contained extra insights of a person who checked facts to the point of becoming personally involved with events. While searching for the real story, he was always concerned about getting too consumed by his work.

Fes had tried marriage once. This attempt led quickly to a divorce because he realized he was too tied to his work and she was involved with someone else.

Following his divorce, Fes roamed more freely and distantly. His travels brought him to Colorado. He was not prepared for some of Colorado's "Oh My God" highways that go over mountains, rather than around them, and have a sheer drop on one side with no guardrails. Such highways in the sky are not designed for people who have a habit of getting preoccupied in thinking about their work while they are driving.

Thinking about an intriguing story, Fes was driving too fast for a turn that was approaching. Gravel was scattered on pavement next to the rock wall on Feston's side of the highway. There was also, on the pavement, directly ahead, an eagle tearing at a piece of meat.

Seeing the eagle, Feston turned his thoughts away from his story and put on his breaks. Tires skidded on loose gravel helping to swerve the car toward a sheer drop on the opposite side of the road. He watched in horror and disbelief as the car turned. He saw the clear, blue sky and felt a floating-dropping sensation before there was an explosion as the car hit the first outcropping.

The vehicle's interior filled with debris. Fes either successfully opened the door or it was torn outward by the impact. After undoing his seatbelt, he jumped from the slowly moving car. It gained momentum and dropped out of sight. Fes heard a crash then another followed by an explosion before a ball of dark, acrid smoke ascended. This moving, snakelike stain in the sky diminished to become a tendril that gradually dissipated.

Being a person who didn't like heights, Fes knew he must not look down over the ledge. He fought a rush of panic that caused his mouth to become very dry and his heart pounded rapidly. He realized he would lose his struggle against fear if he sat down and let his fears grow so he started stepping slowly along the outcropping.

He was encouraged by the discovery of animal tracks marking sandy sections of the ledge. If animals can walk on this ledge it might lead me off this cliff, Fes said to himself. I think mountain goats or Bighorn sheep have made most of these prints.

He forced himself to keep moving. He knew if he took too much time to think about his situation, he might be overcome by fear. He pushed onward, almost recklessly. I'm moving too quickly, he warned himself. However, just being here is dangerous. Speed might help me to escape from nervous tension. I can use my nervous energy. Tense nerves are causing me to tremble and fumble. I don't want to get too clumsy. Although I'm shaking slightly, I'm still in control of my actions. Maybe I'm moving quickly enough to stay ahead of my fear.

Fes pushed ahead and almost rushed onward. He wanted to think the outcropping was getting wider. He didn't want to have to go back. If there isn't a way out o' here in either direction, I'm really going to face a desperate end, he thought. Trying not to consider anything other than the ledge, he kept stepping forward as rapidly as possible.

When the outcropping widened sufficiently for him to relax and rest, he sat down. He was sweating and exhausted. Fear shook him. The blue vastness in front of him was so worrisome he forced himself to keep walking. He resumed his steady pace although he started to move more slowly and cautiously.

In spite of an overwhelming drive to get off the ledge, fatigue eventually forced him to stop. He sat down on a sandy section of the path. Becoming drowsy, he stretched out, pushed his back against the rock wall then slept fitfully.

He woke up facing the moon. He felt even more confined at night because he couldn't see the ledge clearly enough to walk. He had a sensation of being trapped in the sky with the moon and stars in front of him. He clung to the rocks and welcomed sleep.

When he woke up again, sunlight was brightening the edges of a tendril of cloud. His side of the mountain was cloaked in shadows. At least I know the directions, he noted. I'm obviously facing west.

Dried blood remained on his hands from small cuts caused by grasping the rock wall as he walked. He resumed traveling, pushing onward until he came to a widening in the outcropping of rock. Relief washed over him when he was able to step away from the cliff's edge. The world regained some normality.

An eagle soared effortlessly passed the mountain. Fes could clearly see the bird's alert, yellow eyes. Frost outlined some of the bird's feathers. The eagle must've come down from a great height, thought Feston. During this trip, I didn't know my companions would be eagles. When I get back to solid land, I'm going to stay there. I'll leave these high places to other people and eagles.

Fes observed that another of his constant companions was fear. This fear was worrisome. He tried to fight off more fear when he saw the malicious, yellow eyes set in a whitish face. Beyond this whiskered face, there loomed a tawny body. Muscles bunched and rippled under thick fur as the animal approached Fes.

Feston knew his dread of the cliff's edge was much greater than any concern he had about a cat. This cougar would have to turn back because I can't retreat, Fes thought.

How unlucky can I get? Fes asked himself. There must be only a small number of mountain lions in Colorado and I have to meet one along a narrow route. Of course, I'm the intruder here. The ledge is a place where a cougar would live. It would come here to try to stay away from people.

Terror jumped in Feston when the cat screamed. The tawny animal shot out another piercing scream, then Fes picked up a rock. His other hand gripped a second rock. I fear the open emptiness beside me more than any cat, Fes reminded himself while the animal stepped closer. The paws were wide with long claws.

The cat moved quickly, partially immobilizing Fes with terror. He almost just watched instead of reacting to the attack. Springing off the ground and darting through the air, the cat's jaws were open and paws outstretched before Fes, tightly gripping a rock, swung it forward. The rock hit the cat's head, knocking the animal sideways into blue space. After being silhouetted against a blue haze for an instant, the tawny form dropped out of view and left Fes staring at the sky. His heart was pounding so loudly he thought every creature and person must know that Feston Tucker was standing alone on a mountainside.

Feeling triumphant after escaping from the cougar, Fes resumed walking. His feeling of elation gave him extra energy. He pushed onward a little carelessly and slipped on loose gravel. When his feet shot out from under him, he fell on the ledge, leaving his legs kicking in space. Struck by fear again, he clawed at the rocks until he got a firm grip on a protrusion. Pulling with his hands while kicking with his legs, he scrambled away from the precipice. I hate heights, he exclaimed to himself after he sat down with his back shoved firmly against the mountainside.

Looking into a menacing expanse of clear, blue sky, Feston said to himself, if I get off this ledge, I'm going to be more careful with my life. I've come so close to death here, I'm going to start considering life to be more precious. I've faced my own death and scrambled away from it. I've been given another chance. I have an opportunity to do things differently. With my second chance, I can go back and do some fixing. The one thing I would change would be my attitude. In my new, second life, I'm going to be more adventuresome. I'll take extra chances and simply be more aggressive. I'll put my new assertiveness to work immediately by getting busy rather than waiting here any longer.

Fes started walking again. The exhilaration he experienced through getting a second chance at life received a setback when the ledge petered out. Fear, his old enemy, returned as he looked ahead and saw how narrow the trail had become. Although the ledge had narrowed, the mountainside had changed from a sheer drop to a more gradual slope. Below the ledge he had been following, there was another, wider outcropping. It led to an almost flat area containing tall trees.

I might be wise to deliberately slide to that lower section, rather than wait until I fall to it, thought Fes while observing the terrain. I'll be happy to leave my present ledge and return it to mountain lions and Bighorn sheep. There must be mountain goats here also although I haven't seen any.

Feston knew if he delayed for too long, he might talk himself out of any kind of bold action. He was not going to change his decision to be more assertive with his second life. He had to drop to the wider trail so he braced his boots against rocks below the ledge. With both hands, he grasped adjacent rock ridges. Slowly, he eased himself over the edge. Almost instantly, he lost control of his momentum and plunged along the wall. Jagged rocks scraped his back before he slammed against the lower ledge. Pain exploded through him, leaving him numb and almost unconscious. He had fallen mainly on one leg, dislocating the kneecap. The dislocated kneecap bulged grotesquely under the skin on one side of his knee. The unnatural sight of this displacement was almost as sickening as the pain gripping his whole body and filling his mind. He sensed a whispered roaring sound in his head.

In a numbing, somewhat delirious, state of bone grinding pain and terror, he put his hand on his kneecap and pushed. When it wouldn't move, he punched it. It slipped back into place with such pain he screamed and lost consciousness.

He woke up in sunlight then moonlight of passing days. Searing pain in his leg gradually subsided to a steady soreness. The pain in his back lessened although, with his fingers, he felt a gash and in it things were moving. Flies have left me with maggots, he told himself. He dreaded the implications of having maggots living in his back. They caused an itchy feeling.

Feston thought he had reached the bottom of his life when he saw the bear approaching. At first he saw the entire animal. As the creature came closer, Fes could only see the legs. The large paws had surprisingly long claws.

Well, I don't have to worry any more, Fes thought while again he faced the prospect of meeting death. He was too weak, sore and tired to fight a bear. Pressing his face against the rock ledge, Feston covered his head with his arms. He remained motionless when the bear was close. Fes could hear the animal breathing. Its breath smelled of fish. Teeth tore material on the back of Feston's shirt and jacket. A damp nose and sharp teeth brushed against the skin on Feston's back. The animal's wet, strong probing tongue started licking out the maggots. The removal of maggots stirred an overwhelmingly pleasant tickling sensation. Fes fought the urge to move. He grimaced quietly and remained still, pushing his face tightly against the rocks. The bear smacked its jaws loudly. Upon finishing the maggots, the animal continued walking along the path, leaving Fes feeling very grateful to not have been injured again or killed.

The bear must've been eating fish and wasn't very hungry, thought Fes. All the creature needed was a few tasty grubs. Fes relaxed then welcomed sleep.

The next morning, he stood up and felt no pain other than a general soreness. Trying not to bend his injured knee, he worked his way to the protective cover of lodge pole pines. He rested here before pushing onward. He was exhausted and sweating when he reached the creek. It was a tumbling, mountain stream and he welcomed its thirst quenching water.

After removing his clothes, except for his underwear, he stretched out in the chilling stream. He let it numb his sore and tired body. Piercing cold provided soothing relief to the pain in his leg and also his back.

Shaking from the cold, he stepped out of the water then removed a lighter from the pocket of his jeans. He worked hastily, almost feverishly, to assemble a pile of kindling. Using his lighter, he started a small flame among the finest twigs. Flames climbed among sticks, flickered along larger chunks and gradually formed a steady, crackling blaze.

Fes basked in the fire's warmth. He also used sand and water to wash his clothes. When they had dried beside the fire, he put on the heated, clean clothing.

He felt well and almost contented except for being hungry and having a sore knee. To prepare for hunting he first selected a sharp stone. He used it as a crude axe to cut down a sapling that would provide a suitable spear. This weapon, particularly its point, was hardened in flames.

Feston made a collection of spears, thinking that, if he got into additional trouble, he might need more than one. The creek seemed to be the best place to start looking for food.

He quickly discovered he could not distinguish outlines of fish in swiftly flowing water. He had to follow the stream's bank until he reached a pool of calmer water. In this more placid, and thereby clearer, water, he was able to see the forms of trout. They were facing upstream and resting in the stream's current.

Fes threw a spear at the fish. The shaft whooshed over the trout, clunked against the pebbled streambed then floated on the surface. The fish darted away like shadows only to regroup again in much the same locations. Three more spears were thrown without hitting these elusive forms. A fifth spear was aimed below its target and wounded a trout. As it struggled, its sides flashed tints of silver and pink. Fes stepped into the water and caught this fish. He also collected his floating spears. Afterward, he moved his fire to the edge of the pond.

I have a fine camping place here, he said to himself before he skewered the fish on a spear. He positioned this trout above the flames until the meat turned a golden brown color. Upon completing sufficient cooking, he pulled away the crisp skin then removed moist chunks of meat. This food was tender, juicy and delicious, having an added smoky flavor.

Life is looking better, reflected Fes as he licked his fingers. I have cold, clear drinking water along with roasted trout. This is a beautiful place for a camp. The mountainside and trees provide shelter from the wind.

Evening shadows darkened the forest and patterned the pond. Firelight sparkled on the edge of the water. In another shadowed section of the water's surface, there was a clear reflection of the moon. It, at first, had a reddish tint. Colors faded while the moon climbed the sky. Eventually, a silver sheen of moonlight lit the land, etching the forest's floor and pond with an intricate tangle of lights and shadows.

Time seems to be of little importance here, reflected Feston as he sat beside his fire. This place hasn't changed much through the centuries. I could be in any century now. Maybe I could do a story about this forest being an enduring wilderness. The land has thrived without human interference. A forest lives better by itself without human attempts at management.

Having sipped some cold water, he said to himself, of course, I have to get back to the highway. However, that's not such an easy thing to do. I can't climb up the mountainside to get to the road above me. I haven't seen any lights or heard traffic sounds in front of me. All I can do, I suppose, is try to walk along this mountainside until I come to another road or a more accessible section of the highway. If I travel far enough, I'll reach something. My knee is sore but I can use it if I don't bend it too much. I think my back has healed. It isn't sore and doesn't itch any more. I suppose the bear enjoyed the maggots. I was lucky to get rid o' them.

Feston Tucker slept beside his fire. In the morning, he felt cold in addition to being hungry. I think I'll try to spear a few more fish and get well rested before leaving my comfortable camp, he told himself. I want to let my leg heal naturally without any setbacks.

Picking up his spears, he checked the trout and was relieved to see they hadn't changed their general locations. The fish continued to be bunched in the current, particularly where it entered the pond. Each fish was facing upstream and resting in the cold water. The first spear hit the pebbly streambed, scattering the trout. In a short time, the fish started returning to the current. A second spear hit a shadowy form. Rainbow and silver hues flashed from the fish as it struggled upward then splashed on the surface, sending ripples across the pond. Fes stepped into the water. He caught the trout then picked up his spears.

Skewered on a spear held above the fire, the fish roasted quickly, providing a delicious meal. I've enjoyed my camp beside this pond, Fes thought while savoring the last of the smoke-flavored meat. My leg has healed sufficiently for me to walk as long as I move slowly. Although I can't bend my knee much, I can get around well enough to catch a wounded fish.

Feston slept soundly through the next night. At dawn, he started walking down the forested mountainside. The misty air was scented by a fragrance of pine. Fes carried his spears and used one as a walking stick.

Because he had come close to being killed on the cliff, he was more appreciative and observant of beauty in life than he had been previously. Now that I have a second, and even a third, chance at life, I'm going to fix things I was doing poorly the first time, he thought. I'm going to appreciate life more and I also must be more assertive. During my first life, I didn't notice its beauty sufficiently. I was too content to be a watcher or recorder of life rather than a participant.

When he came to an expansive meadow, he felt worry trickle through him, leaving him with a cold empty feeling. He had located a large crop of marijuana. There's trouble here, he warned himself. The people who planted this crop aren't going to want visitors. I definitely can't go back and I don't want to risk walking through this stuff. I'll move beside it and try to get away from this meadow as soon as possible. I'm tired. I don't want to re-injure my knee. Therefore, I'll go into the woods, find a secluded place then make a camp. I would also like to find some food although I don't know what there would be to eat around here.

Hearing voices in the distance, Fes moved as quickly as his sore knee enabled him to get across rough terrain. He found a secluded place to make a camp. He kept his spears ready for use although they wouldn't protect him very well against people with guns. He decided that for his own safety he had to remain hidden and stay away from people.

Having selected a site concealed by trunks of ponderosa pines in addition to rocks, Fes risked the preparation of a small, smokeless fire. It provided warmth and helped him to rest; yet he needed food.

An eerie stillness gripped the forest. Evening shadows deepened, bringing a night that was quiet until an owl hooted.

Feston was alerted by the sound of a twig snapping or a branch breaking. This noise seemed menacingly loud in the forest's solitude. He picked up a large stone and, with his other hand, he gripped a spear. He heard bushes rustling. A twig or branch snapped again.

Looking back along his own trail, Feston saw a dog approaching. With its head down, sniffing at scents, the animal was walking steadily toward camp.

Maybe the thing's friendly, thought Fes. This hope vanished when he recognized the sleek form of a Doberman pinscher. It growled and advanced steadily. Since there's one dog, there could be others, Fes warned himself. Hearing a tapping sound of feet hitting the ground, he turned to face another attacking dog just as it sprang upward. Fes swung the rock, hitting the dog's lower jaw. There was a snapping sound as the jaw broke. The animal was knocked backwards but regained its footing quickly and charged in a reckless rage. Fes put all his strength into a spear thrust to the neck, killing the animal.

With a spear ready, Fes turned toward the first dog that had been approaching almost mechanically. Continuing to growl, the animal hesitated, stopped, then rushed forward. Fur bristled on the dog's neck. Snarling viciously with eyes clouded, the thing attacked meeting an upward piercing spear. The shaft entered the dog's throat. After a few gasps, the dark form slumped to the ground. I'm sorry about the dogs, thought Fes. I like them except when they're trying to kill me. Of course, that's not their fault. They've been trained to attack intruders. I won't be able to sleep now. I'll just keep traveling and see if I can get out o' this region.

By staying away, as much as possible, from trees and following the edge of the marijuana crop, Fes could distinguish forms clearly enough to see where he was walking. An overhead canopy of moon and stars provided pale light.

Since there's a gang in here growing marijuana, there should also be a road, reasoned Fes. That road will take me back to the highway.

In the night's stillness, he was startled to hear the sounds of voices. People were talking ahead of him. Next, he heard the sounds of boots tapping against the ground. Two people are talking as they are walking toward me, observed Feston before he stepped behind some bushes.

Ahead, he saw a light. That light isn't moving, he said to himself. There must be a camp in front of me. I wouldn't want to get caught by these people.

Continuing to listen for sounds, Fes saw a moving spark. Two people are walking toward me and one of them is smoking, thought Fes. They won't see me. I'll just remain hidden and they'll walk passed me. There's a road here. It'll take me to the highway.

"When the ol' man dies, we'll use his cabin as our headquarters," said one of the two men who were approaching Feston's position.

"We've broken his legs so he won't be goin' anywhere," replied the other man. "He stays in his cabin most o' the time anyway. Ol' Cliff Kellar's a strange sort o' guy. He came here to die so we don't have to kill him. We've just tried to hurry things a little. We don't want him to get out and talk too much. His cabin will be more comfortable than our tents. There's no need to kill him because he's goin' to die anyway."

After the men had passed Fes, one man stopped to light another cigarette. The small flickering flame from a lighter lit the cigarette while illuminating a whiskered face. The flame was extinguished then the lighter was returned to a pocket. An ember on the cigarette brightened when the person inhaled smoke. He blew the smoke toward the bushes where Feston was concealed. Afterward, the man kept staring in the same direction.

Fes thought he could feel the stare. This can't be happening, he thought while his heart seemed to be pounding much too loudly. His mouth dried as fear crept through his tensed body. This guy will turn and walk away, Fes said to himself. They have to keep walking. They have guns.

The guy didn't turn. He started walking directly toward Fes.

The man had seen something and was going to investigate. There was no way of avoiding trouble so Fes pulled back a thick branch and released it. When it whacked against the man's face, he screamed with pain and shock. He bent over, holding his face. The other person shot once, sending a bullet over Feston's arms before a spear sank into the gunman's crotch. A piercing scream came from the speared man then he gasped for breath and sank to the ground. Both men dropped their rifles. Fes picked them up. He kept one, threw the other away and started walking along the road.

I don't think they'll be chasing me right away, thought Fes. They don't have guns. One man has a problem with his face and the other guy has a problem with his crotch.

Hearing more sounds of boots tapping against the roadside in front of him, Fes stepped behind a thicket of brush. After two men passed his position, he continued walking. He proceeded to a camp concealed by camouflaged coverings. Only one light appeared from a tent under the patterned canopy.

I should've maybe walked the other direction, thought Fes. However, I was heading in this direction before I came upon the camp. I'll get out o' here more quickly if I stay on the same route rather than turn back or keep changing courses. There's another light ahead. Maybe it's coming from the ol' guy's cabin. I'm tired and weary. I can't risk getting into any more trouble with the men behind me. Possibly Cliff Kellar would tell me how to get out o' this mess. I can't risk making mistakes. I must know what road to take and the direction I should be heading. I'm tired and hungry. Cliff Kellar might help me and I could help him. He's my best hope right now. I can't just wander around when gang members are hunting me. They presently don't know anything about me and that's good.

While Feston walked toward the light, a cabin's outlines became more distinct. The light came from a window in a log building.

In front of the cabin, there was a log bridge built over a creek. While Fes was crossing this bridge, he noticed a person watching him from a darkened window at the far end of a room where an oil lamp illuminated another window.

Upon approaching the front of the building, Fes tapped his spear against the door. Hearing no response to the first knocking, he again tapped his spear against the door. Maybe I'm making a big mistake here, he warned himself. Likely I should just keep following the road and see if it will lead me out to an highway.

Fes heard someone, or something, move inside the building. Next, he saw a man sit down on a chair located beside a table containing the lamp. "Come in," shouted the man.

Feston opened the door. He stepped into a partially lit room. Turning, he found himself facing a pistol held by a white-haired man reclining in a chair beside the lamp. The lamp was on a roughly hewn table. Both of the man's legs were bandaged in straight positions. The legs must have been broken. Crudely constructed crutches were on the floor next to the chair. This man's blue eyes sparkled behind glasses. In the remainder of his reclining body, however, strength seemed to have seeped away. He held a gun and this gave him all the strength he needed for the moment.

Feston's appearance was something that would worry anyone. His hair was tangled. He was tall and seemed to be strong enough to concern an opponent. His clothes were torn. A rip in his jeans revealed some material used to wrap one knee. Furthering his rough appearance, he carried a rifle in one hand and a spear in the other.

"What kind o' jackass are you supposed to be?" demanded the white-haired man.

"Well, I suppose I might look like one; but I'm not trying to be one," replied Feston. "Are you Cliff Kellar?"

"Yeah," stated the man. "And who would you be?" he asked gruffly.

"Feston Tucker," he answered. "I'm a newspaperman and I usually work out o' San Francisco."

"And what would you be doin' around here lookin' like that?" asked Cliff, continuing to point his gun at this intruder.

"Farther up the mountain, the highway went one way and my car went the other, takin' me over a cliff and here I am. I'm lucky to be alive. I've almost been killed a few times. Right now, I'm tryin' to get back to the highway and I thought you might be able to help me with some directions. Over by the tent camp, I heard some men talkin' about you."

"Are you with them?" asked Cliff.

"No," answered Fes. "I had a fight with two o' them. They'll be lookin' for me. I don't think anyone saw me come in here."

"Close the door and lock it," said Cliff.

"Okay," replied Fes before he leaned his gun and spear against a wall. He pushed the door to close it then locked it.

"I was makin' tea over in the kitchen," explained Cliff, pointing his gun toward the opposite end of the room. He placed the gun on the floor beside his chair before adding, "You could serve the tea. You'll find another cup in the cupboard." When Fes stepped toward the cupboard, Cliff said, "The guys at the tent camp broke my legs. You can serve tea faster than I can. That tea's supposed to be good for all my ailments. The guys outside are expectin' me to die and the sooner the better. I don't think I'll be disappointing them."

In the kitchenette, Feston poured tea into two cups. He took one to Cliff while leaving the other on a table beside a chair closer to the doorway. Afterward, Fes added pieces of firewood to embers in a fireplace located on the north side of the room. As flames crept upon this wood, he sat on the chair facing both Cliff and the fire.

"Thanks for getting the tea," said Cliff. "I've been waitin' for one honest person to come by this way before I died. Do you think you might fit that description?"

"I've been known to be honest from time to time," replied Fes after sipping some tea. It had a refreshingly pleasant flavor. "Actually I try to be honest all the time."

Enjoying the chance to rest with warming firelight brightening the room, Feston said, "There's a fragrance of burning leaves in here. Do you burn anything other than wood?"

"Yeah," answered the older man. I burn marijuana in the fireplace, occasionally, for medicinal reasons of course." A smile brightened his lined face before he added, "The stuff makes me feel better, maybe. I seem to have a lot o' ailments that I don't intend to bother you, or myself, about. I have other things for you to do."

"Can you tell me how to get out o' here without running into tent-city again?" asked Feston.

"Yes," answered Cliff. "There's an old logging road that continues on passed my cabin. This lane will take you to a real road and it connects with the highway. There's a gas station and a general store at the junction. You could call a taxi from there."

After sipping tea, Cliff explained, "The gang members keep me cut off from the outside world. They took my truck and broke my legs. I guess they see no reason for killin' me because that isn't necessary considerin' my lousy state o' health. This place is also my home now and I'm pleased to stay here. They bring me supplies; but, of course, they've also taken everything. They've taken my land."

Upon drinking the remainder of his tea, Cliff said, "You could get us more tea because I have work to ask you to do."

Feston took both empty cups to the kitchenette where he refilled them. He gave Cliff's cup to him and returned the other to its place on the table beside the chair. Fes added a log to the blazing fire that was filling the cabin with welcome warmth. He sat down and relaxed before sipping the mildly flavored drink.

"Thanks for getting the tea," said Cliff. "Now that I'm at the end of my road," said the older man, who seemed to be energized by the green tea, "I've had time to look back at my life. Upon reflection, I find that there're two things, in particular, I have to fix before I leave. This is where you come in. I've wanted to meet someone who could do two things for me. I can pay for such work. You only have to agree to help me and you have to be honest."

"I'll do this for you if I can," answered Fes.

"My real home," continued Cliff, "is in the Uinta Mountains of northeastern Utah. In these mountains, there's a gold mine. Spaniards forced the Indians to work at this mine until the Indians rebelled and drove the Spaniards southward. Brigham Young and the Mormons also worked at the mine. The mine either, for some time, stopped producing gold or the Indians traded for iron pyrite from a mine in Arizona and Brigham Young thought the iron pyrite came from the Uintas. Either a shortage of gold or the presence of iron pyrite caused Brigham to abandon the mine. Members of my family started working in the mine and I have a deed to the land. I have gold from this Uinta mine. I also worked at the mine in Arizona.

The southern location was the iron pyrite mine. The Indians used iron pyrite for decorations. I had a partner, called Zackery Tomkins. He found a gold mine that had been worked by the Spaniards. My partner thought the Spaniards were driven away or killed by Apaches before gold could be removed from the mine. Zackery started working all the time at his new mine. Meanwhile, I got tied in with his wife, Rita. I left with Rita and we went to my property in the Uintas. We had one daughter. Her name is Candice Kellar and she lives in my house beside the mine in the Uintas. We ran a trading post beside the mine. My so-called wife, Rita, left with a trapper and I haven't heard from her. My daughter's boyfriend, Redge Osburn, was a lazy, good-for-nothing type and I couldn't convince my daughter to get rid o' him. I had a couple o' fights with him and, in time, one of us was going to kill the other. This situation wasn't helping me get along with my daughter. I got fed up with the trouble and bought land here. I was quite content until tent-city moved in and started growing marijuana. By the way, I've been talking so much my throat's getting dry. Where you thinking o' makin' more tea?"

"Yeah, okay," answered Feston as he stood up. He walked to the kitchenette, turned on the gas stove, refilled the pot and boiled water for steeping tea.

When each man was sitting down again holding a cup of steaming tea, Cliff said, "You will be wondering what my story has to do with the work I have for you."

"Yes," replied Feston, not wanting to get into any more trouble too quickly.

"Well," continued Cliff, "I was wondering if you would help me fix the two outstanding mistakes I've made in my life?"

"If I can, I will," replied Fes. He drank some flavorful tea then waited for the other man who seemed to be in no hurry to finish his story as if ending it might be getting him too close to the end of his life.

"As I've explained," said Cliff, "I have devised a way for you to correct two mistakes I've made. If you will first go out to the back of the wood shed, you'll find a stepladder. Bring the ladder here and stand it up in the center of this room."

Fes went outside, found the ladder and carried it into the cabin. He stood the ladder up in the center of the room.

"Climb the ladder," said Cliff. After Fes had managed to get half way up the ladder, Cliff said, "Push on the ceiling boards until a trap door opens."

Pushing against the ceiling, Feston moved a board. He applied more force to the loose section and a trap door opened. He kept it moving upward until it leaned against a beam and stayed open.

"You'll find a flashlight on the attic floor near the trap door," directed Cliff. "If you don't mind climbing up there, use the flashlight to help you see where you're going. At the far end o' the attic, above me, you'll find three canvas bags. They're in the midst of a lot o' other stuff. Please bring me the three bags."

Being careful with his sore knee, Fes managed to get through the opening and crouch on the attic floor. He saw the flashlight located near the base of the door. Upon picking up this light, he used it to check the contents in a musty chamber. The air was stale and permeated by a slight fragrance of pine resin. Roughly hewn logs, topped by boards, formed a low, tent-like room containing two trunks along with extra equipment.

Fes moved slowly to the section located above Cliff. I wonder if I'm a fool for coming up here, Fes thought. Maybe the man's legs aren't broken and this whole thing is some kind of a trap.

Behind a section of partitioning, Fes saw three canvas bags, or haversacks. Picking up one, he was surprised to find it was quite heavy. The second container had the same weight, as did the third. Looping the straps of the containers over one shoulder, he carried them to the trap door.

Making three trips, Feston brought the haversacks to Cliff. "Thanks," said Cliff after the work had been completed. "I couldn't have done that myself. Please put the flashlight back where you found it, close the trap door and replace the ladder."

"Okay," replied Fes. He put the flashlight on the attic floor near the base of the trap door. He closed this door then returned the ladder to the back of the wood shed. When he entered the cabin again, Cliff said, "Were you thinking of pouring more tea?"

"Okay," he replied. He poured the tea, served it, then sat down thinking he must have finished his work.

"Thanks for your help," said Cliff after sipping the green colored tea. "If you accept the job I have for you, you'll be taking these three bags with you." Pointing to one of the containers, Cliff added, "For your payment, you will keep the first bag. Take it now and look inside."

Feston got the haversack and took it to his chair. Upon sitting down again he opened the bag and, inside, he was surprised to see gold nuggets. "Looks like very good payment," he exclaimed. "What do you want me to do?"

"At first, I planned to do everything myself," explained Cliff. "As my health deteriorated, I prepared for someone else to deliver these packages. Of course, when my legs were broken, I was handicapped further.

After I came here, I had time to look back and think about my life. Upon doing this, I realized there were particularly two things to fix. Thereby, you will be delivering these two other packages. I found I had one, outstanding regret, along with the two things I could at least attempt to correct. My plan required the locating of one honest person to make the deliveries. You're sure you are honest enough for this assignment?"

"If I can carry out your plan, I will," replied Fes although he was a little worried about what kind of a mistake he might be making.

"After I've explained the work involved, you can, of course, accept the job or reject it," explained Cliff. "Don't take on the project then steal my money. Although I haven't made many friends, I have learned that most people are decent. I also seem to have an ability to judge a person quickly and accurately. I think you're a decent person and also an honest one. Because my health has deteriorated, you're now exactly the person I've been waiting to find. Fortunately, I've been able to find a person like you before I died."

"If I'm capable of doing this work for you, I'll do it," replied Feston.

Pointing to one of the containers on the floor beside him, Cliff said, "We come now to the next haversack. It contains a map with directions leading to a place where I used to live in Arizona. Near my house, I poked around in a mine containing only iron pyrite. The Indians used it for ornaments. I had a partner there and, as far as I know, he still lives in the house. As I've told you, his name is Zackery Tomkins. He was working in a mine nearby. I mentioned to you it had been used by Spaniards. According to his theory, Spaniards had pushed into the region and, for a short time, took the mine from the Apaches. Apaches used gold to trade for supplies. Zack believed the Spaniards had been driven away, or killed, before they could remove all their gold from the mine. I'll get to my point now and stop repeating myself. Maybe saying everything twice comes with isolation. If Zack has found gold, don't give him the nuggets I have for him in this pack. He only gets these nuggets if he needs them. If he doesn't need money, his gold will be added to the third pack. I had gold set aside for Zack because I took his wife with me when I returned to the Uintas. All of this gold has come from the mine and my home in the Uinta Mountains."

"I can do that for you," said Feston feeling somewhat relieved by these requests.

"Good," stated Cliff. "Now we get to the third bag. I've mentioned to you that Rita and I had a daughter called Candice. Rita later took off with a trader, or trapper. Candice continues to live at my house in the Uintas. Inside the third container, I have included a map explaining how to get to my place in the Uintas. The bag contains gold for my daughter. There's also a deed for the property. Please give the deed and gold to my daughter. Tell her there are precious stones such as rubies and diamonds inside pottery bowls located in the mine. Don't give anything to her so-called husband, Redge Osburn. He's a short, slim, wiry guy with long, brown hair, prominent cheekbones and brown eyes. His mouth usually has a smile on it although his eyes remain serious and calculating. He latched on to my daughter because of the business and its money. I've never understood women and my daughter doesn't understand men."

"That's the whole assignment?" asked Feston.

"You have it," confirmed Cliff. "By giving gold to my partner, if he needs it, I can relieve my conscience a little on that topic although, when I left with his wife, I didn't realize how much I was helping him. He should be feeling sorry for me and maybe he does." For the first time, Cliff's features brightened as a smile crossed his face. "My daughter," he added, "will need help because she's staying with Redge Osburn. I knew if I shot the guy my daughter would turn against me and trouble was looming all around me so I left and came here. After building this cabin, I wasn't feeling well. I went to an hospital and didn't like what they told me. The gang members that moved here haven't been very helpful either. However, only my own mistakes really concern me and I'd like to correct two of them as I have told you."

"I'll take care of your packages for you just as you have requested," said Fes. "Upon looking back on your life, you said you had one other regret."

"Yes," answered Cliff. "When I came here, I had time so I read the bible and have become a Christian. I regret the fact I didn't become a Christian sooner. Belief in Christ brings us back to God, rather than having us wandering away. Decisions that take us away from God also lead away from what's best for us. Things or events leading toward God bring us closer to what is best for ourselves and this leads to our personal happiness. With these three bags I'm sending out with you, I've made my peace with God and myself. My mind is now at ease and I can rest as long as you are honest and deliver the packages as you say you will."

"I'm honest and I'll deliver your parcels for you," affirmed Feston. "Are you sure you want to give me this bag of nuggets?"

"Yes," replied Cliff. "The work, to me, is worth the pay and much more. I thank you."

"Can I write about this story some day?" asked Fes.

"Yes," answered Cliff. "You can write about my story as long as you're kind to me and my daughter. Don't cause any trouble for us. I won't be around much longer for trouble or anything else to find me. I'm more concerned about my daughter."

"That's the only way I'd do the writing anyway," replied Fes.

"You are welcome to make yourself at home here," said Cliff. "You can sleep on the chesterfield and there's food in the kitchenette."

"The marijuana growers are looking for me," said Fes. "If they find me here, there'll be trouble for both of us and I might not get your packages delivered. Maybe I could take a few cans of food, along with a spoon and can opener then I'll start walking along the old logging road. I don't want to cause you any trouble and I have work to do."

"You sound like the right person for the job," stated Cliff, obviously pleased. "You're welcome to stay; but I'd also like to see you get my work done."

"Could I take a few cans o' food?" asked Fes.

"Take what you want," answered Cliff.

"I'll put a few cans in this container you gave me, and thanks for the generous pay—in advance," said Fes as he stood up. He got the three bags and took them to the kitchen. "The bags are heavy but not too heavy," he told Cliff.

"Food's in the upper and lower cupboards," said Cliff. "There's a knife drawer there too."

"Thanks," replied Fes before he opened a cupboard door and removed four cans of beans. From the knife drawer, he obtained a can opener along with a spoon. "This will be great," he said, "because I can't carry much and you're going to need all you've got."

Cliff stood up using his crutches. "Thanks for your help," he said. "An honest man is worth his pay. I hope you don't get into any trouble. If you get into any difficulties, I'll have to send out another messenger to apologize to you." A smile crossed his tired face.

"Any trouble I get into will be my own fault," stated Feston as he opened the door. "Thanks for the work."

"Thanks for the help," replied Cliff. After stepping outside and closing the door behind him, Feston hastened to conceal himself among shadows.

He hurried along the lane. Upon traveling a short distance, he stopped beside some bushes and remained still while he listened for sounds of pursuing enemies.

No worrisome rustlings disturbed the solitude. Cliff Kellar has relied on me to correct two things in his life, reflected Fes. In selecting me for such work, he, of course, didn't have much choice. I was likely the only person available for the job. He also correctly sensed I could be trusted. I'll certainly carry out his instructions. He knows I'll do these two things for him. I have to deliver two messages. One parcel goes to Zackery Tomkins in Arizona and the other is taken to Candice Kellar in Utah. I'll have to deliver the message to Zackery first because he gets the gold only if he needs it. There's no sense in giving gold to a person who already has enough—or more than enough. I must complete these two tasks then I can get back to my own work.

Feston resumed walking. Moonlight lit the route sufficiently for him to identify outlines of the terrain. I'm tired and hungry, he thought. However, I'd like to get away from the gang before I rest. I have my own safety to think about and I have a responsibility to deliver these packs. As a writer for newspapers and magazines, I've always worked to uncover the truth in a story. Previously, I have managed to not get too involved in the story. This time, I've become a participant in the news. I must not let myself get involved to such an extent again. I've been more accustomed to remaining an observer of life. Maybe that was my personal mistake. Cliff Kellar is correcting things in his life by getting me to deliver two messages. I have resolved to be more aggressive or assertive in my life; but I should continue my policy of not getting too involved in the news. I hope I can keep such a distinction. Maybe more assertion in my personal life will get me more involved in my stories. I must keep walking and reach the road then the highway. Cliff said there was a service station and general store at the junction of the road and highway.

Feston's thoughts were interrupted when he heard the sound of a vehicle coming behind him. Immediately he left the lane and stepped behind some bushes. While he waited in the still, partially moonlit forest, worries crept through him. Until now, he said to himself, I didn't think about the fact I might be leaving boot prints along this lane. Even if I have left easily detected prints, the men would have no way of knowing who had left such tracks unless they could be compared to marks made where I got into that scuffle. If these men are following my tracks, I'm going to have problems.

The vehicle advanced slowly. Feston was relieved when a jeep passed his position. Now I have two men in a jeep in front of me, Fes told himself. If the men are just looking around and not following tracks, I have nothing to worry about. He felt a flash of fear when the vehicle could be heard returning.

One man walked ahead of the jeep. He was looking for boot prints that had turned off the trail. I've got a real problem now, thought Fes. I can't run because I have a sore knee. If I stay here, they are going to find me. Maybe they'll pass me again and figure they've driven over the tracks and erased them.

Feston shoved the packs under the branches of a spruce. This action alerted the approaching man. He stopped, raised his rifle and fired a burst of shots. Bullets whooshed over Feston's head, spraying him with pieces of wood and spruce needles.

Following the shots, both men advanced to see what had been hit. Fes didn't move although his heart was pounding and he was sure the men would hear it. They walked passed him. Maybe I could get back to the trail, Fes thought. I have to get my packs. He moved to get the bags and pulled them from under the branches. Upon standing up, he turned to leave and found himself facing guns held by the two men.

"This is the same guy," said the man who had been following the prints.

"That was good tracking," replied the other man. "I didn't know you were a tracker."

"I'm an hunter," said the man. "I also had a reason for wanting this guy. He put a spear in me and I'm goin' to put one in him."

As the man spoke, he reached for the spear held by Feston. Rather than surrendering the weapon, as expected, Fes shot it forward and upward. Screaming with pain and rage, the man held his crotch and fell forward. Fes, continuing to hold the spear, shot it sideways at the other man's face and spoiled his aim. Bullets raked through treetops before the spear hit the man again across the side of his head. He slumped to the ground.

Feston felt exalted, realizing he had faced death another time and escaped. Keeping one gun and spear for himself, he threw the men's other weapons into bushes. He recovered the packs, pulling their straps across his shoulder. He walked to the jeep, placed his packs, gun and spear in the back then sat on the driver's seat. After turning the vehicle around, he drove slowly along the poorly defined lane.

Feston drove the jeep until it got stuck in ruts. He left the vehicle and continued walking. The first gray light of dawn helped him detect the route of the logging lane. He was relieved to see it wind toward a paved road.

Fes followed the shoulder of the paved road until exhaustion forced him to look for a place where he could rest. He walked along a creek bank and stopped in a grassy area. He stretched out on dry, grassy ground under a ponderosa pine and welcomed sleep.

When he woke up, he found himself looking at an intricate network of overhanging branches. Beyond these branches, there was a starlit sky. Moonlight dropped a tangled web of shadows across the forest's floor.

Fes walked to the stream. He drank refreshingly cold water. Not wanting to risk building a fire, he got the can opener, opened a can and savored spoonfuls of cold beans. I haven't had a meal for a long time, he said to himself while using the spoon to remove the last of the beans from the can. I must resume traveling. I'll have to be careful because the gang will be hunting for me.

He continued traveling. Each time a vehicle's lights appeared, he stepped behind bushes or trees and waited until the vehicle had moved out of view. Distances seem much farther to me because I'm not only walking with a stiff knee but I'm also carrying these bags, he reminded himself before turning away from the road and sitting down to rest with his back leaning against the trunk of a ponderosa pine. He opened a second can of beans then chewed them slowly.

He started walking again and was relieved when he saw a light ahead. I'll call a taxi to get a ride to town, he said to himself.

Being both exhausted and dirty, Feston opened the door at the garage. Sitting on a chair behind a cluttered desk, a man was sipping coffee from a paper cup. He had a grayish beard with balding hair and dark eyes. He wore a green uniform and thought the guy at the door was one of the dirtier drivers although there had been others in worse condition.

"Do you know where I can get a room at this time o' night?" Feston asked, displaying money in his hand.

"There're rooms at the back—and showers," answered the bearded man. "We also have washing machines and dryers."

"Thanks," said Feston. He received a key, paid the man then hastened to one of the small, driver's rooms. He first enjoyed a long shower. Afterward, he purchased new clothes and threw out his other clothing. He also bought sandwiches along with coffee at the service center. His life seemed to be getting back to normal.

The next day, Feston took a taxi to the closest dealership where he could lease a truck. He put his share of the gold in a safety deposit box at a bank. He also withdrew extra cash from this bank. For most of his traveling expenses, he intended to use credit cards. He completed all necessary purchases for traveling, equipping himself for some camping and cooking. After all his supplies had been carefully packed, he started driving southward to deliver the first package to Zackery Tomkins in Arizona.

SEVEN

ARIZONA MINE

I'm going to try to not get too involved with the people or their situations when I deliver these two packages, thought Feston Tucker as he crossed into Arizona. He proceeded steadily onward and, according to the map, from the haversack, the preferred stopping place was the motel at the Cameron Trading Post in Cameron.

Feston rented a room at the motel then entered the restaurant where he ordered the local, favorite food called Indian Taco. It consisted of a large piece of round, fried bread covered with chili, peppers, tomatoes and onions. This food was one of the tastiest meals Feston could remember savoring. He accompanied the taco with coffee. He sipped coffee slowly while he enjoyed the rich, timeless atmosphere of Navajo culture in the restaurant.

The waitress was an attractive woman with short, black hair and dark eyes. She wore a long, red dress with a silver belt. When she was refilling Feston's cup with steaming coffee, he asked, "Do you know this region well?"

"I should know it," she answered.

Showing her the map, Fes listened intently as she described the route marked by a red line extending northeastward to the mine. "That area is very isolated," she said. "I don't think anyone lives there except, according to your map, Zackery Tomkins. I've heard about a prospector who lives alone out in a valley. He must be Zackery Tomkins. That name sounds familiar. He is on Navajo land; but he doesn't bother anyone."

"If he found gold, how much of it could he keep?" asked Fes.

"The prospector would keep some and the Navajo government would keep part," she answered. "This prospector is a friend of yours?"

"He had a partner called Cliff Kellar," replied Fes. "Cliff Kellar asked me to visit Zack and see how he was getting along."

"That guy might be hard to find," she said. "I've heard about him a few times. There's a wide area where he might be. The first place you will come to is an abandoned house. He lives east of this house. I think you can drive to the house. I've just heard about these things. I haven't been there myself."

"Thanks for your help," Fes said before she walked to the kitchen.

She returned with the bill. Placing it on his table, she said, "Good luck with finding Zackery Tomkins." Smiling, she added, "He might be a ghost by this time."

"Thanks for the thought—and the information," he replied.

She walked toward people at another table. Feston left a large tip on his table before going to the entranceway to pay his bill. He purchased some extra maps in the trading post then returned to his room.

After checking his maps and thinking about Zackery Tomkins, Fes slept very little. He finally stopped trying to sleep. He packed his equipment, stepped out of his room and walked to his truck. He drove northward, crossing the bridge over the Little Colorado River.

A pale moon dropped a ghostly sheen on a landscape containing magnificent shapes and contours. Rocky summits became more clearly outlined against a backdrop of a brightening sky. First rays of sunlight emblazoned the pinnacles. This light moved down the slopes and lastly swept along plains and valleys. Contemporary houses along with traditional hogans dotted the windswept land. Horses grazed in addition to sheep.

Fes stopped a few times to get food and coffee. He kept traveling and, among night's shadows, he slept in his truck.

At dawn, he was traveling again. According to the map, he was on the right road although, by the appearance of the landscape, he wasn't on a road. The route had dwindled to a few, remnant vehicle prints. He thought he might have become completely lost until he saw the abandoned building.

Sheep tracks marked earth around a pool next to a well. The house had collapsed into an elongated pile of boards topped by a broken roof.

Feston drove passed the house and proceeded eastward until he came to a valley bordered by distant, rocky summits. He followed a zigzagging course to avoid obstacles such as cacti along with rocks and clumps of creosote bushes or mesquite trees.

Each time Fes came to a dead bush or tree, he put firewood in the back of his truck. By nightfall, with shadows lengthening grotesquely across the land, he had acquired a large supply of wood for his campfire.

He perked coffee at the fire's edge. He also roasted wieners on a stick held over the flames. Lastly, he heated beans in a can. When cooking had been completed, he sat on an outcropping of rock and slowly savored a tasty meal of beans, wieners and coffee. Following this meal, he refilled his cup with dark, rich coffee and sat down again to relax while he watched a shadowed land beyond the flickering fire.

He sipped coffee and let it stir his thoughts. So far in my life, he reflected, I've managed to be a partially successful newspaperman. I've written enough stories to make a living at this type of work. I work mainly out of San Francisco although I have to keep traveling to get stories. Now I'm looking for a ghost in a land of shadows under a pale moon. There's nothing tieing me down to any particular place aside from the newspapers and magazines in San Francisco. I'm going to help fix Cliff Kellar's life by delivering two messages. I've decided to change my own life by being more assertive or aggressive. Previously, I was too much of a watcher of things. Now I plan to take part and be more active. Before I had the car accident, I would have gone this far on a journey then turned back. According to my present, more assertive, lifestyle, I'll proceed onward. I'm driving a truck along this valley and I have only a vague map to follow. I think Zackery Tomkins is in the next valley to the east. In the morning, I'll continue driving through this valley until I reach the rocks. I'll probably have to walk across that height of land and Zack's camp should be in the next valley, or somewhere on the other side of the eastern summit.

An owl hooted repeatedly. The calls rang clearly through the still night. Later, coyotes called, then silence followed. Feston slept in his truck.

Dawn cast a red hue on the valley and eastern rocks. Feston rekindled his fire and fried bacon followed by eggs. He enjoyed a fine meal and sipped coffee as he watched sunlight move down the pinnacles.

I'll try to drive to the rocks today, thought Fes. I will have to walk across the summit and look for Zack on the other side. If I don't find him, I will at least have tried my best and gone as far as I can go. During my previous way of looking at life, I might have turned back already. Now I'll go to the other side o' those rocks before I quit. I can then say I carried out my obligations. By this time, as the woman at the restaurant said, Zack could be a ghost.

After breakfast, Fes started driving, collecting firewood each time he passed a dead tree or bush. He followed a winding route, trying to avoid cacti, rocks and bushes.

He was close to the rocky summit when the back of his truck dropped down and the tires started spinning. He accelerated forward, then backward, in a desperate attempt to dislodge the vehicle. He felt a thump and the truck stopped moving as tires kept spinning.

He stepped out of the vehicle and walked back to check the tires. I can't believe this is happening, he exclaimed to himself incredulously. The truck is resting on its axle. Of all places to get stuck, this is the worst. I'm as far away from any road as I intended to drive. I was going to park the truck here—or close to this place—and look for a way to walk passed the rocks.

Shock and disbelief mixed with a flash of anger as he continued to survey his predicament. One back wheel had dropped into a long, narrow hole.

He was getting into the back of his truck to find a jack when his foot, that was still on the ground, slid into an opening behind the tire. He fell backwards, scraping his leg as it descended farther into a cavity in the earth. His other leg was jerked off the truck, straining his sore knee.

Sprawled on the clayish earth, he rested, trying to control his rising anger and settle his nerves. I've been winding and zigzagging across this valley, he thought. I suppose getting stuck was always a possibility. Dropping into some kind of an hole, just when I was going to stop driving, is so frustrating. Worrying won't help.

Fes stood up. Although his knee was sore and his other leg was scraped, he managed to pull the jack from the back of his truck. Working slowly and carefully, he used the jack to raise the vehicle. He placed a rock under the raised axle then repositioned the jack in order to continue lifting the truck. Eventually, he was able to shove slabs of rock, along with chunks of wood, across the hole and under the tire.

Starting the truck again, he felt many of his worries vanish when the vehicle lurched forward onto firm ground. He thought the world had returned to normal as he stepped out of the vehicle and proceeded toward the depression where the tire had become stuck.

Upon removing pieces of wood and rock, he noticed pebbles as well as particles of earth dropping into the hole. On each side of this opening, there was wood. He removed more earth and was amazed to discover a large, dark cavity bordered by logs on two sides. Fascinated by this discovery, his curiosity kept him working almost feverishly. He was sweating as he pulled a log out of the ground. More earth dropped into an enlarged hole then the ground collapsed under Feston's boots. He scrambled frantically to break his fall but failed to get an hold on anything solid. With a shower of earth and rocks, he tumbled into a vast hole and fell under a cloud of clayish sand.

His flailing arms had helped to slow down the speed of his descent before his back slammed against the bottom of a dark cave. Snakelike tendrils of sand continued to flow from the broken ceiling, adding to an haze of dust in the damp air. Fes closed his eyes and covered his face with his shirt. He was able to breathe through this material.

After the air had cleared sufficiently for him to remove the shirt, he opened his eyes and, above him, he saw a patch of bright, blue sky. Surrounding this piece of sky, there were jagged edges of a ceiling about eight feet above a sandy floor.

I must've dropped into some kind of a sinkhole, he told himself. It could've swallowed my whole truck.

He tried moving and was relieved to feel no further pains. The fall hadn't broken any bones or strained more muscles.

Gradually, his eyes adjusted to dim light. He realized he was in a small chamber. A darker area on one side appeared to be an opening to a connecting room.

Feston stood up. Upon selecting a piece of wood from the chamber's floor, he used his lighter to ignite a splintered end. Firelight flickered across straight-sided walls in addition to ceiling beams topped by earth.

He stepped toward the darker area and discovered it was an entrance to a second room. Flickering light from the burning stick shone on metal bars stacked in a neat pile.

Picking up one bar, Fes was surprised by its weight. He tapped the metal against a rock imbedded in a wall under the broken ceiling. Each hit put a small dent in the bar.

Feston had been sweating before he fell into the chamber. Stale, earthen scented air increased his sweating. His heart was pounding with the realization of what he had discovered. Heavy, soft metal has to be gold, he thought. I've stumbled into the gold cache that Zackery Tomkins has been looking for throughout most of his life. The Spaniards didn't hide their gold near their smelter. The gold was smelted beside the mine. Gold bars were cached here. Zackery Tomkins must not have found anything.

When a coiled thing dropped onto Feston, he sprang back in sheer terror, thinking he was entangled with a rattlesnake. Expecting a snake, Fes stared at the round, thick coils moving on the room's floor. Horror turned to surprise as he found himself watching a stirring rope. This rope was looped on the floor and extended up to the break in the ceiling. This opening was partially covered by a man's head. The head spoke, saying, "You can use that rope to get out o' there, or I'll come down."

"Who are you?" asked Feston.

"I be Zackery Tomkins," answered the ghostly face. "Who are you?"

"I'm Feston Tucker," replied Fes. "I was sent to look for you."

"I'm not down there," exclaimed Zack. "I'm comin' down though as soon as I tie this rope to somethin'."

The head vanished from the opening, allowing more light to enter the rooms. Much light was blocked again when Zack reappeared and climbed down the rope. "What are you doin' here?" asked Zack. His voice was raspy.

"I fell in here," answered Feston. "My truck got stuck in an hole. I was checking the hole and fell into it myself."

Zack lit another piece of wood. His eyes looked wildly around at light moving across beams and clay walls. He was a roundly shaped man with stooped shoulders. He had gray, tangled hair and a flat face with brown, red-rimmed eyes.

Zack walked into the adjoining room. Fes followed him and watched him pick up one of the bars. "I've spent my entire life lookin' for this," Zack exclaimed as not only his eyes but his whole face looked wild. His burly features were accentuated grotesquely by firelight coming from the burning wood. "When I find it, you're here," he added unpleasantly. "Are you goin' to try to claim this?"

"I inquired about this sort o' thing," answered Feston. "We are on Navajo land. They'll be claimin' most o' what is found on their land. The rest will go to you because without you none of this would've been found. I was just lookin' for you and fell in here by accident. If I'm going to get a share, a finder's fee, I won't turn it down."

"All that seems fair enough to me," said Zack.

Feston was greatly relieved to know the man was going to be reasonable. An hole in the ground was no place to have a serious argument.

"I'm just pleased to finally see the gold after all these years," said Zack. "I was findin' nothin'. I was afraid all my years o' searchin' were goin' to come to nothin'."

"Well the gold's here and I'm sure you're now a rich man," said Feston.

"I feel grateful to you," said Zack. "You'll get your share."

"How did you get here anyway?" asked Fes.

"I have a place just over the hill," Zack replied. "You were makin' so much noise over here I had to come and see who was trespassin'. I saw your truck. I saw the ground just swallow you. You just vanished. I know I've been alone too long but I didn't think I was getting that bad. I came over and saw the hole in the ground. I looked down and there you were. I went back and returned with a rope. So that's how I got here. Did you say you were lookin' for me?"

"Yes," answered Feston. "I came here looking for Zackery Tomkins."

"Well, that's me," exclaimed the wild looking man. "Why would you be lookin' for me?"

"Cliff Kellar sent me to check on you," said Fes.

"Oh," replied the old man, as he seemed to slump somewhat. "That name takes me back a long way. Cliff Kellar was my partner—and I had a wife, Rita. My partner ran off with my wife. Maybe I should say my wife ran off with my partner. She was never much of a wife anyway. And I guess I could say he wasn't much of a partner."

"You're probably right about your wife," said Fes, "because she also left Cliff and went away with a trapper or trader."

"That's not surprising," exclaimed Zack. "Of course, I wasn't up to much either if I was to be completely honest about the whole thing. I spent all my time lookin' for this gold that I didn't find until you found it. Someone's always runnin' off with my stuff. First, someone takes my wife, and now my gold."

"Well, as I told you," answered Fes, "I'm not taking anything. This is Navajo land; therefore, the gold belongs to them. Some also belongs to you. You'll be rich. If I get a finder's fee, I won't complain."

"I'll see that you get your share," said Zack. "I'm grateful to you for finding the gold. I never thought o' lookin' over here. I've been diggin' at the mine for years an' years. If you hadn't come along, I wouldn't have found anything so I'll see that you get your share."

"When I leave, I'll notify the Navajo government," said Fes.

"Yeah, they'll straighten this all out," replied Zack. "They'll be pleased to get their share and I'll be pleased to get my share. You leave me—and them—your name and address and your share will come to you."

"We should start things off by getting out o' this hole," said Fes. "You tied the other end of this rope to my truck?"

"Yes," answered Zack.

"Go on up," said Fes. "I'll follow you."

Zack, then Fes, climbed up the rope. They were relieved to get into fresh air and sunlight. Staring at the surrounding landscape, Zack said, "Things turn out very strangely. If my wife hadn't run off with Cliff, he wouldn't have felt guilty and sent you to check on me. Therefore, you would not have found the gold and I would never have received anything. So if we start to think about things, we maybe find that everything is goin' around in a big circle. I should thank my wife for leavin'. If I ever see her again, I'll thank that cheatin' woman with all my heart."

"Do you do a lot o' thinking?" asked Fes, amused by the man's point of view.

"I've had a lot o' time to think— when I'm not digging," he answered. "Say, you'll have to come over for dinner. My cookin' is clean—even cleaner than I am." He added the last remark smiling crustily.

"I appreciate the invitation," said Fes. "However, maybe I should invite you here for dinner because someone should watch this gold.

After spendin' so much time looking for the gold, you don't want to risk losing it now."

"Well, you do have somethin' there," said Zack. "How clean's your cookin'?"

"Much cleaner than I am," answered Fes.

"Pleased to hear that," said the old man, laughing.

"Do you always live out here by yourself?" asked Feston.

"Of course not," said Zack. "A coyote visits me all the time. I feed ravens. I have an old truck and I drive to town now and again. I have a postal box in Cameron. I get mail and government checks. The government invested in me when I was broke. I'll now be happy to invest in the government. I'll be pleased to be able to pay taxes again. More taxes mean I'm makin' more money."

Feston quickly prepared kindling for a fire. He ignited this wood then added larger pieces. He placed the coffeepot at the fire's edge to get the coffee perking before he started frying bacon. He also heated beans in cans. Lastly, he fried eggs. This food was served on paper plates accompanied by plastic knives, forks and spoons. Basic garnishments were ketchup, salt and pepper.

Serving Zack a plateful of steaming food, Feston said, "I hope you like beans."

"I must like them," he answered as a grin furrowed lines on his face. "I have them every day."

"Well, we wouldn't want to miss a day, would we?" replied Fes while he prepared to pour coffee.

"No, of course not," answered Zack. "I really wouldn't want to miss coffee for a day. The bacon and eggs, though, are special and thanks for all this food. I haven't seen such a fine meal since I was in the restaurant at the Cameron Trading Post."

"This should just be the first o' many fine meals now that you're rich with all the gold," said Fes. "When I leave, I'll notify the Navajo government so people will come here and sort things out for you. I'll also leave my name and address in case there's a finder's fee."

"I'll protect your finder's fee," stated Zack. "I still can't believe you'd come here and find the gold that I've been lookin' for all my life. Of course, by the tire tracks you left windin' around the desert, you probably didn't miss many places."

"I was tryin' to avoid all the obstacles so I wouldn't get a flat tire or drop into an hole," replied Fes.

"You did very well," said Zack. "I thank you for coming here and saving my life because I would never have found the gold if you hadn't got stuck on top o' the cache."

Upon finishing this meal, both men sat on the ground, leaned their backs against the truck and drank coffee. "I've had lots o' time to think about mining," said Zack. The mine next to the house produced iron pyrite. The Indians used it for ornaments. Later, the Indians used gold, from the mine where I've been workin', to trade with other people who were arriving, bringing new trade goods like guns.

When Spaniards came here, they would have shot at the Indians so the mine could be worked. The Indians would have been Apaches or Navajos.

Spaniards couldn't carry ore; therefore, they made a crude furnace to smelter the ore and form the gold into bars. The bars could be taken south. The mining operation was out in the open. Thereby, the gold—or most of it—was hidden here. The Spaniards must have planned to take some gold bars with them and they would return later for the other bars stashed in this cave.

Something went wrong, obviously. The Indians either killed all the men at the mine, or killed most of them and drove the others away. I've found human bones in at least three different places. In one skull, there was an arrowhead.

Cliff Kellar's family knew about the pyrite mine because the Indians were trading pyrite and the Kellars were interested in mines—or prospecting. Cliff Kellar has family property in the Uintas. This property includes a mine that was worked by the Spaniards, then by Brigham Young and the Mormons. The Kellars got some gold—the last of it—from the Uinta mine.

Not many years ago, I went to the Uinta mine to see what had happened to Cliff Kellar and my wife, Rita. The only person I met was someone I didn't like. He said his name was Redge Osburn. He was a short, scrawny guy who was livin' with Candice Kellar. I got into a fight with this guy and he just about killed me. He had a knife in me before the fight started. If you're plannin' to go to the Uinta mine, don't trust that guy at any time."

"Thanks for the advice," said Fes.

"You said you were lookin' for me and that's why you've been drivin' around getting stuck," said Zack.

"That's right," replied Fes. "I'm a reporter—writer—doing newspaper work mostly. I was drivin' my car in Colorado and went off the road."

"That's easy to do in Colorado," added Zack.

"Yeah, so I discovered," said Fes. "My car went farther down the cliff than I did. I managed to stay on a ledge. I walked down the mountain and ran into some people who were growing marijuana. I also met Cliff Kellar. He had gone there to live in a cabin. Rita had left him in the Uintas and he didn't get along with Redge Osburn. Cliff isn't in good health. Upon looking back at his life, he regretted two things in particular. He was sorry he left with your wife, Rita. He was also worried about his daughter, Candice. Cliff wanted me to give you some gold nuggets if you needed them."

Fes walked to the driver's door, opened it and reached behind the seat. He removed a pack then gave it to Zackery. "I was told to not give you these nuggets if you already had money. You are going to get a share of the gold in this cave. But getting your share of the gold is going to take time and I think you've waited long enough. You need money now so I'm giving you this package that Cliff Kellar sent to you."

Receiving the pack, Zack said, "I guess good things happen if we wait long enough. I figured I'd be dead before I got what I wanted." Opening the pack and taking out some nuggets, he exclaimed, "Thanks. You could've kept these nuggets for yourself and Cliff could've kept them too."

"Cliff sent them to you," replied Fes. "I got the job of being messenger because I was the only person available and I said I was honest."

"You kept your part o' the bargain and Cliff has tried to keep his part after all these years," said Zack as the lines in his face deepened. "You're right though," continued Zack. "Getting money out o' this cache could take a lot o' time and I've waited long enough. If I wait any longer to get paid, I'll be dead."

"You have your message and my work has been done," said Fes.

"Yeah, thanks," said Zack. "You got more accomplished in one day using a truck than I've done in a lifetime with a pickaxe. But at least the work has been completed and we've all had a part."

"I have come to believe our life's quality or success is measured by how we do things more than by the things we actually get accomplished," said Fes.

"Yeah, I hope you're right," said Zack. "I've lived my own life honestly and haven't hurt anyone."

"That's the best we can do," replied Feston.

"I'm mightily pleased to see you're livin' your life honestly too," Zack added, flashing a rare smile

"Yes," said Fes. "I've received more gold by giving it to you rather than by keeping it."

"Yeah," exclaimed Zack. "I've received more gold too because you didn't keep it and I really appreciate it. Now that I have some money, I'm goin' to start takin' life a lot easier. I'm going to try to really enjoy all the pleasures an' comforts I've missed."

"I should start traveling while I can see where I'm going," said Fes.

"I have to go back to my mine," said Zack. "I'll get some supplies and come back here to watch our gold until help arrives."

"I'll notify the Navajo government when I leave," said Fes. "I've enjoyed meeting you," he added, shaking hands with Zack.

"This has been a good day for me," said Zack. "I've received good news from everyone except Rita."

"I'm going to the Uintas next to give a similar package to Candice," explained Feston. "Do you have any messages for anyone? I seem to have become some kind of a post office."

"If you see Cliff, thank him," replied Zack.

"Any messages for Rita or anyone else?" asked Fes.

"No," answered Zack. "She made her own decisions and they didn't include me."

"Enjoy your money," said Fes before he stood up and put away his equipment. Having finished this work, he got into his truck. "You've earned that money," said Fes, speaking through the truck's open window.

"I'm going to enjoy it," said Zack. "I'll probably go to town, buy some luxuries, then come back and live here where I've been all these years."

"If I see Cliff again, I'll tell him this part of his life has been corrected," said Fes.

"Yes," answered Zack. "He has done his best."

Feston started the truck and turned it to follow his previous, winding route. There was still enough daylight remaining for him to visit the Navajo government and get help for Zackery Tomkins. Afterward, Feston had one more package to deliver and this work would bring him to the Uinta mine.

EIGHT

UINTA MINE

Feston Tucker notified the Navajo government about the gold cache being guarded by Zachery Tomkins. After taking care of commitments to Zack, Fes headed north to the Uinta Mountains.

The mountains were much more beautiful than he had imagined them to be. While beholding a wide sweep of forested slopes, he thought, I'm going to use my share of this money to buy a section of land beside the San Joaquin River. I'll purchase a remote site in the mountains and build a log house with a fireplace. From such a location, I can send my work to San Francisco.

Following the map included in the pack to be given to Candice Kellar, Feston drove to the site of the Kellar homestead. The building was a sprawling structure. Dark logs indicated the original section. It had been both an home and a trading post. This building had been expanded with lighter colored logs to form a bar and a restaurant. Cabins were nestled among ponderosas an each side of the main structure. When Feston parked his truck in front of the bar, he noticed that a car and a truck were parked next to the older part of the building.

Fes left his truck and stepped up onto a veranda. From here, he proceeded to open a screen door, then a wooden door. Closing these doors behind him, he entered a spacious room with a rustic atmosphere. Wooden tables and chairs filled most of the south portion of this room. Along the south wall, there was a large, stone fireplace. The north wall contained a bar with stools located in front of a long counter. Behind this counter, there were shelves of bottles backed by a large mirror that was as long as the counter. The northeast corner was an open entranceway leading to the kitchen.

Feston walked to the counter and sat down on a stool in front of a woman who was working in a small office behind a cash register. The woman had black hair colored by a light, brown tint. Her eyes were brown. Although she looked disinterestedly at Feston, he noticed that she was definitely attractive. "What would you like?" she asked.

"I'd like to rent a cabin—your most isolated cabin—on the south side, if you have one for rent," he replied.

"I'll put you in number eight," she said while working with a computer. "It's the farthest back among the trees. How many nights?"

"One," he answered. "If I can stay longer, I'll renew each day."

"Okay," she said. "Do you want anything else?"

"The breakfast special if it's still available," he replied, pointing to a breakfast notice written on a blackboard, listing coffee, sausages and blueberry pancakes.

"All right," she said before walking to the kitchen. She returned almost immediately and placed a cupful of steaming coffee on the counter in front of Fes.

"Thanks," he said. "Is the coffee any good here?"

"It's the best," she replied. "It's made from pure, spring water."

"Are the pancakes any good here?" he asked.

"They're the best because they're made by me," she said.

"They have to be good then, don't they," he said as she returned to the kitchen.

Fes took his coffee to a table. He sat down on a chair next to the table. From this location, he could watch most of the bar and also look out through an eastern window to see his truck.

There's no need to rush anything, he thought before sipping the strong, rich coffee. All I have to do is deliver this last package to Candice Kellar then I'll get back to my own work and build a new log house near the San Joaquin River. If I ask too many questions right away, I might scare away the right answers. I could get some rest. I'll poke around and deliver my message at an appropriate time.

The woman brought Feston a plateful of steaming pancakes accompanied by thick sausages. He topped the pancakes with butter followed by syrup. The pancakes had a wheaten flavor mixed with a bittersweet taste of blueberries.

"Coffee's good," he said when the woman refilled his cup.

"Thanks," she replied with a smile brightening her face.

"Pancakes are the very best," he added.

Her eyes brightened as she turned away and took the coffeepot to the kitchen. She returned and placed a key on his table. "This is for cabin eight," she said. "If you're stayin' longer you can let us know. You're the only one here so there shouldn't be a problem getting' your cabin for additional nights."

"You have my bill ready?" he asked, standing up.

"Yes," she answered. She walked ahead of him to the bar.

Feston paid his bills for the meal and cabin then walked outside to check his truck. He left the bag of gold hidden behind the driver's seat. Lastly, he made sure the vehicle's doors were locked.

Carrying his supplies to his cabin, he moved into the place quickly. The cabin had been constructed entirely with logs. A kitchenette contained cooking supplies and food staples such as coffee. Wood was neatly stacked beside a fireplace. More wood was piled on the porch.

This place is perfect, he thought while his lighter sent a small flame climbing among kindling. A steady flame was soon blazing across large pieces of wood. Nothing good has ever come to me easily, reflected Fes after he sat down to rest in his new home. I'm going to like living here for a while. I'll deliver this last package to the right person then I'm going to build my home beside the San Joaquin River.

Hearing a knock on the front door, Fes said, "Come in." The door opened and the woman from the bar stepped into the doorway. "You're findin' everything to be okay?" she asked. "You're our only guest so I thought I'd make sure you're satisfied."

"This is a perfect cabin," he replied. He had a feeling about this woman that made him want to keep her company. He also sensed her aloofness as if she preferred to stay away from people as much as he wanted her to remain. "I'm surprised—although pleased—there aren't more people here," said Fes. "We must be in the slow season."

Her eyes paled before she said, "The bar wasn't a good idea. The bar has caused trouble and scared off other, regular guests. The mountains are magnificent. The history of this place is as contradictory as our present situation. In the great beauty of these mountains, we've had trouble. If you were thinking of sitting out on the veranda, I could come back and tell you a story."

"I was thinking of sitting out on the veranda," replied Fes.

"I'll be back soon," she said before turning away from the doorway and walking toward the bar.

Feston was sitting on one of the chairs on the porch when the woman returned. She was carrying two paper cups filled with coffee. Sitting down on a chair next to Fes, she gave him one of the cups and said, "I'm having a rest." She had not realized she had been lonely until he arrived.

"You aren't overly busy here," Feston said after tasting the coffee. It was strong and rich. "Thanks for the coffee."

"As I said before, we haven't been busy since the bar was added," she replied. "Our guests who liked peace and quiet didn't like the bar. The people who preferred the bar didn't want to come here because it was too quiet. I enjoy a quiet place. The mountains are magnificent. This is my home."

"You're a good cook," observed Feston.

"I had to learn how to cook because no one else wanted to do it," she said.

"You seem to be doing everything—looking after the restaurant, bar and cabins," said Fes.

"There's another woman here and she does the housekeeping," she replied.

"And you do everything else," added Fes.

After sipping coffee and watching a squirrel running along the branch of a ponderosa, she said, "This property includes an abandoned mine. Spaniards forced the Indians to work in the mine until the Indians rebelled and drove the Spaniards southward. Brigham Young and the

Mormons continued the mining. They either thought they had run out o' gold or thought they had started getting only iron pyrite. The Indians traded iron pyrite and much of it came from a mine south o' here in Arizona. My father worked at the Arizona mine before coming here with my mother. My mother, Rita, had been married previously to my father's partner, Zackery Tomkins. My father is Cliff Kellar. He brought my mother here because this was his real home."

"What's your name?" asked Feston.

"Candice Osburn," she replied. "When you registered, you put your name down as Feston Tucker."

"Yes," he said.

"You just came here for a rest?" she asked.

"Yes," he answered. "I do investigative writing for newspapers mainly based in San Francisco. I am getting some rest now then I'm going to buy land and build a log home in the mountains near the San Joaquin River. You're married?"

"Yes," she replied, looking down.

"Your name was Candice Kellar?" he asked.

"Yes," she said, gazing up with a serious look on her face.

"Do you have any kids?" he asked.

"No," she answered. "You ask a lot o' questions," she stated as her face clouded, showing some annoyance.

Fes said to himself, she's a private person and I've intruded too far and too quickly.

"If you stop asking all these questions, you can have a cigar," she said, giving him one she had been keeping out of view beside her. She kept one for herself.

"Thanks," he replied, accepting the cigar and reaching for his lighter.

She used a match to light her cigar. A wisp of smoke drifted away from an ember on the tobacco and she said, "I like the company of a cigar. When I'm by myself, quietly smoking a cigar, I can think best."

"You do a lot o' things for company," he said without thinking. "I bet you got married just for company."

"And what business would that be of yours?" she snapped with her eyes flashing.

"I thought we were friends," he countered.

"We are, maybe, if you watch what you say and ask," she stated. Anger had flashed through her and dissipated much more slowly.

"I thought, with friends, it was possible to say and ask things without worrying," he said.

"Maybe so," she replied carefully. "Although I don't always like what you are saying—or asking."

"I ask and say things not to be mean but to get information or to give other people a chance to explain their points of view that I'm not sure about myself. That's what I do. I get information and write about it—in a way that does not harm anyone."

"Is that what you're doing now?" she asked with annoyance clouding her eyes. "Are you just getting information?"

"Yes," he replied, even surprising himself with such honesty. "However, I'm getting information because we're friends. If we weren't friends, I wouldn't care what you were doing."

"Oh, I see," she said. A dark, serious look seeped into her face and she watched him carefully.

"What's your husband do?" asked Fes.

"Nothing really," she answered. "He works at the bar sometimes." She looked at a distant summit of the mountains. Gazing back at him, her eyes were serious.

Candice did not see the man approaching because he had left the back of the bar and was walking toward the cabin. Watching the man, Feston steeled himself for possible trouble. Noting the change in Feston's face, Candice knew her husband was approaching. "I'll be getting back to work," she said. She stood up, turned away, stepped off the porch and started walking toward the restaurant.

"Aren't you goin' to introduce us?" the man asked Candice. He was short, slim and wiry with long, brown hair and dark, brown eyes. His face was smiling although his eyes were serious.

"No," she answered as she passed him.

"I'll have to introduce myself," he replied while he kept advancing. He stepped onto the veranda and said, "I'm Redge Osburn. Who are you?"

Fes felt instantly irritated by this man's intrusion into what had been an happy moment. Fes had been warned about Redge and hadn't liked him even before seeing him. The appearance of the man, coming at a time when Fes was within the spell of the woman's company, was infuriatingly unwelcome.

"I'm her husband," said the man.

"Oh," replied Fes.

"Yeah," he said, smiling maliciously. "I'm her husband."

Feston felt increasingly repelled by the insertion of this man's unwelcome presence. "Yeah, you said that before," stated Fes.

"I say it twice to people who spend too much time talking to her," he said, grinning.

"What else do you do?" asked Feston, willingly crossing the line to check this annoying intruder.

"I get rid o' people who get in my way," he stated.

"Well, good for you," said Fes, having decided to not be bothered with this annoyance.

"I'm goin' up to the bar now," Redge continued. "I'm goin' to get your payment. I'm goin' to bring it back here an' you can get ready to leave."

"That's why there are no customers at this lodge," exclaimed Feston, thoroughly angered. "No one else can stand havin' you around."

Fes saw Redge's hand move to the back of his belt. The hand reappeared, holding a knife. The blade snapped open. There was no forward rush. The knife flash was a display meant to intimidate.

When the knife was pointed at Fes, he kicked it. The kick came so quickly and unexpectedly that the knife was dislodged from Redge's hand. The blade flashed upward and stuck in the side of Redge's face. Screaming, he pulled out the blade. Blood gushed from the cut and dripped across his clothes. Enraged, Redge rushed forward clumsily.

Fes opened the screen door, swinging it swiftly, using all his strength. The door shattered when it slammed against Redge's head. A blank expression crossed his eyes, the knife dropped from his hand then he slumped onto the floor of the veranda.

Feston removed a first aid kit from his pack. He sprinkled alcohol along the cut in Redge's face before applying a bandage. Afterward, Fes walked quickly to the restaurant.

Candice stared worriedly at Fes as he said, "He came at me with a knife so I kicked the knife. When it was knocked from his hand, the blade flipped upward and stuck in the side of his face. He grabbed the knife, pulled it from his face and lunged at me so I opened the screen door and slammed it against his head, knocking him out. I put alcohol along with a bandage on his cut. I'll help you take him to an hospital."

Candice looked at Fes steadily for what seemed to be a long time before she said, "He's been cut before and hasn't gone to the hospital. You've put alcohol on the wound and bandaged it. That's what I've done in the past. He'll never stop trying to get you though. I'll return your payment for the room."

"The money was paid for the cabin and I haven't enjoyed a place so much before in my life—aside from Redge, of course—although I was there for only a short time. Do you think I could continue staying here without causing any trouble?"

"He'll never stop trying to get you," said Candice.

"Is it safe to leave you here?" he asked.

"He hasn't hit me," she replied, looking withdrawn and strained.

"I'm going to drive up the road and find a place where I can camp for a while," said Fes. "I'll check back to make sure you're all right."

"Thanks," she replied.

He left the restaurant and walked to the cabin. Redge must have regained consciousness because he was not on the veranda. Working quickly, Fes packed his equipment. He placed everything in the truck then drove to the restaurant, parking in front of the building. When he entered the restaurant, Candice was sitting on a chair beside a table and she was drinking coffee. Seeing Fes, she asked, "Want some coffee?"

"Yes, thanks," he replied. "I'd also like to buy supplies so I can camp farther along the road."

"Okay," she said as she poured coffee into a cup for him. He sat down on a chair at the other side of the table.

"Are you going to make sure Redge is all right?" he asked. "I don't know where he is. He has left the cabin."

"This sort o' thing has happened before," she answered. "We'll just have some coffee then I'll get your supplies."

"Okay," he said. "Sorry for the trouble."

"What trouble?" she asked, staring at him. "I suppose—come to think about it—the trouble has always been here. You just met it. That's all."

Fes knew something had happened between him and this woman that hadn't happened to him previously. "I'll camp farther up the road and make sure you're all right."

"Thanks," she said.

"Of course, he is your husband," he said, feeling angry that this woman, to whom he had become so deeply attached, was living with this guy—any guy. "You picked him. You can sure pick'em."

Staring at him intently, she said, "Yeah, I guess I can. I used to like you."

"You don't now?" he asked.

"I still do—always will—as long as you watch what you are saying," she replied.

"I'll be more careful," he said.

The restaurant door opened and Redge stood in the doorway. Without saying anything, he went back outside. He got into his truck and drove to the road. After turning sharply, the vehicle moved out of view beyond foliage.

"He isn't leaving," said Candice. "He's going to get help."

"Are you sure you're safe here?" Fes asked.

"I'll be all right," she said blankly. "I'll get your supplies. Do you need cooking equipment as well as food?"

"Yes," he answered.

"I'll get everything now," she said, standing up.

"Can I help you?" he asked.

"I'll be all right," she replied.

Candice prepared boxes of supplies while Fes sipped coffee. He walked to the cash register to pay for the bill and she stared at him. "What do I owe you?" he asked.

"You've already paid," she replied. "You can help me put these boxes in your truck."

"Thanks," he answered, before he picked up one of the boxes. She carried another box. He followed her as she walked outside and they placed the packages in the back of his truck. She returned to the restaurant. In a short time, she came back carrying two bundles. "A tent and sleeping bag," she explained while putting these bundles next to the other supplies.

"I'll come back and make sure you're okay," he said. "I'll also return your equipment. If you need any help, I'll be just a short distance up the road."

"A mountain stream crosses the road a few miles north," she said. "This stream flows to a lake. I like the site where the creek enters Clear Lake."

"Thanks," he said. "I'll be there if you need anything."

"See you then," she said as she started walking toward the cabin.

Feston drove northward until he came to a bridge crossing a mountain stream. Just before the bridge, he turned off the road and drove along a fisherman's lane leading to the lake.

Evening's shadows darkened the forest while fading sunlight added a pink tint to the sky and lake. Feston hastily put up the small tent then stretched out the sleeping bag. Next he prepared firewood and finally had time to sit down and enjoy warmth provided by a flickering fire. The sky, lake and forest were being tinted by a deeply pink hue from the sunset. This color became infused by a scarlet tint that gradually turned crimson before these colors faded to become lost among shadows lurking beyond the firelight.

Feston rested while he enjoyed a meal of sandwiches and coffee. I can't stop worrying about Candice being alone with Redge, thought Fes after sipping richly flavored coffee. Redge's mood will be worse than usual although she thought she would be okay.

Fes couldn't stop thinking about Candice and the situation she was facing. Sleeping occasionally and fitfully, he watched much of the night from the side of his fire.

He poured coffee while the moon dropped a shimmering path of light along the lake's calm surface. He enjoyed watching the panorama of forested slopes bordering a lake lit by moonlight. He decided to rest for a few days before revisiting the lodge. Candice said she would be all right. Similar trouble had happened previously.

Feston waited for one day and the next night. He realized he could not really rest and would not delay things any longer. He left his camping place and drove to the lodge, parking in front of the bar. Two trucks he had not seen before were parked in front of the bar and a third was at the back of the building. The car was not in sight. Maybe Candice isn't here, Fes said to himself. There's probably nothing here but trouble.

A woman that Fes had not seen before stepped out of the restaurant and closed the door behind her. She nodded to Fes and walked to the closest, southern cabin. She had dark, blue eyes and long, blond hair. Her hair, combed to the back of her head, was tied with a blue ribbon. She wore a denim shirt and jacket along with jeans tucked into boots.

Feston entered the restaurant. "Hi Fes," said Redge who was sitting on a chair beside a table. He was drinking coffee. He had apparently just finished breakfast because a plate, accompanied by a knife, fork and spoon, were on the table in front of him. Three other soiled plates with cutlery were also on the table and positioned in front of chairs. As Fes had observed previously, Redge's face seemed to be smiling although his eyes were darkly serious. "How have you been?" Redge asked.

"I've been wonderin' how Candice has been," said Fes.

"Haven't you been worried about me?" asked Redge. "I'm the one that got his face cut."

"I figured you'd be all right," said Fes. "I've been worried about Candice."

"She isn't here," said Redge, continuing the deceptive grin. "She left shortly after you. I thought maybe you'd know where she was."

"I haven't seen her," said Fes.

"How did you like the blond that just walked out o' here?" asked Redge mockingly. "She's my real wife. Candice just thought she was my wife. She was really nice though. I'm living with Carol. She's the blond. I've had enough o' this place. Candice doesn't even own the lodge because she has no deed. I have the money and I'm leaving with Carol. You might even wonder why I'm still here. Well, I've been waiting for you. Carl and Roy have been waiting for you also."

While Redge was talking, Fes moved out of the way to let a large man enter the restaurant. The man's hair was covered by a red bandana. A black, leather jacket covered much of his sweatshirt. He also wore jeans and boots. His face was bearded and his eyes were black. The man oozed hostility.

A second man came out of the kitchen. Carrying a coffeepot, he refilled Redge's cup. This man with the coffee was slim. He wore a plaid shirt in addition to jeans and boots. The top of his head was balding. Long, gray hair drooped from the sides and back of his head. He had dull, black eyes.

"I would like you to meet my friends," Redge said to Fes. "They've been waitin' for you too. Carl is beside you. Roy got me the coffee. Would you like some coffee?"

"Not now, thanks," said Fes. He was thinking too intensely to pay much attention to the fear and nervousness he felt. "If you're the only one here, I have no reason to stay. I wanted to make sure Candice had not been harmed."

"She's all right," said Redge. "You seem awfully concerned about my wife. But as I said, Candice has gone and I'll be leavin' with Carol. Roy and Carl will be comin' with us also. This place has been losin' money for years. I have all the money that's here now. The only things left are debts. There's no deed. Candice can have all that. That's what's comin' to her. All I have to do is give you what's comin' to you then I'll be glad to get out o' this place. Candice can keep all the debts—and so can you if you're still around. I sure hope you don't

214

have an accident like the one I had. That was awful."

"Yeah, it was, wasn't it," said Fes, trying to stall until he could think of what he could do. "Maybe I'll get a cup o' coffee to take with me."

"Now that's funny," laughed Redge while his eyes remained darkly serious. "You'd think o' getting coffee to take out rather than drink with me." Turning to Roy, Redge said, "Get Fes some coffee."

"Okay," replied Roy. "If you want to play games, that's fine with me." He walked back to the kitchen. Carl waited.

I'm down to two guys now, thought Fes, and the biggest problem is this guy beside me. "Would you like coffee?" Fes asked the man.

Moving to look more directly at Fes, Carl's eyes turned to the pale color of putty. His arm went back to put extra strength into a punch.

Alerted by the color of the eyes along with the coiling arm, Fes saw the blur of movement as the fist shot forward. At the same time, Fes brought a chair up to protect his face and the fist hit the point of an upturned leg. The man screamed with pain and rage. His good hand held his badly gashed fingers while blood flowed, turning both hands to scarlet.

Knowing he shouldn't give this man a second chance, Fes raised the chair higher before pounding it against the guy's head and neck. One leg snapped off the chair and Carl crumpled into a large pile on the floor.

Continuing to hold the effective weapon in his hands, Fes stepped toward Redge. Redge seemed entranced by the sight of an enraged man approaching with a chair. Fes swung wildly at Redge and the chair's impact sent Redge sliding across the floor.

Fes saw Roy's gun and crouched just before a shot blasted away another leg from the upraised chair. Splinters of wood hit the top of Feston's head.

Continuing to hold the chair above his head, Fes ran at Roy. Fes felt the second bullet nick his throat as his foot shot upward, sinking into the man's crotch. Roy groaned and dropped the gun. Fes picked up the weapon, turned around and saw Redge thrust the knife forward in a vicious jab intended to slice part of Feston's head.

Holding the gun firmly, Fes swung his gun-tipped fist at the knife. The gun hit the knife, dislodging it and sending its blade back into the side of Redge's face. He gasped and bent down, holding his bloodied head.

Still grasping the gun, Feston pointed it at the doorway where the blond woman stood. "You have work to do," he said to the woman. "Help these guys get to their trucks. Take these losers out o' here because they're on private property and don't come back."

The woman's face was ashen with shock and fear as she stared at the room. She had expected to see Feston on the floor and beaten. She could not believe that the three other men were down. She walked to Redge and helped him move to the doorway. While Fes watched, Carol got Redge into his truck. She came back and helped Carl walk to another vehicle. Lastly, she stepped beside Roy and managed to get him onto the driver's seat of the third truck. Carol drove Redge's vehicle. She followed the other two trucks and they left the resort.

Feston filled a box with supplies he selected in the restaurant. After making a list of each item taken, he placed this list beside the empty cash register. He put money under the list and got a key for cabin eight before carrying the supplies to his truck. He drove back to his camp, arriving amid the first shadows of evening.

Upon reaching the camp, he kindled a fire then fried a trout he had obtained at the restaurant. This meal was followed with the usual coffee. He relaxed while sipping coffee and enjoying warmth from the fire.

Clouds above the lake were tinted by crimson light from the setting sun. The campfire brightened against a background of darkening shadows.

I have to deliver the package to Candice, observed Feston after refilling his cup. These packages I've had to deliver have had tremendous impacts on my own life. Since meeting Candice, I haven't been able to stop thinking about her. I've tried, right from the beginning, to not think about her because she's married. I have attempted to stop being tied to her. Maybe now, being involved with her, is not such a problem due to the fact she wasn't really married. Redge's actual wife is Carol. She is with him and they have left the lodge. Possibly Candice has also left permanently. I've never been so completely interested in any woman.

Such an interest is not entirely a wonderful thing. Every time my mind is not directly considering some task, my thoughts return to what she might be doing. I have no assurance she's as committed to me as I have become to her. Actually, everything she has done appears to have been against me. I don't think she will come to this camp. To deliver the package, I'll have to wait for her at the lodge because I don't know of any other place to look for her. The lodge has been her home. Maybe, some day, she will return. If I don't wait for her at the lodge, she might go back there then leave again before I have a chance to see her. I must return to the cabin and hope she goes back to her lodge. She will be coming to a lodge that has only debts and no money or deed. Redge won't be there either and maybe she would prefer him to be there. She decided to stay with him previously; so possibly his absence will bother her. I have no reason to believe she would try to see me. Therefore, I'll have to look for her.

At dawn, Feston prepared pancakes, sausages and coffee. Afterward, he packed the equipment, put everything in his truck and drove to the lodge.

The lodge and cabins were ominously quiet. Feston moved into cabin eight. The structure was a comfortable place with one, main room containing a fireplace at the south end along with chairs, tables and a chesterfield. The north side had a kitchenette. The eastern portion of the cabin had a separate bedroom next to a washroom.

Fes built a fire in the fireplace. I'll just stay here until Candice returns, he thought. I'll keep adding to the list of supplies I take from the restaurant and pay the extra money when I see her rather than continue leaving money in the restaurant. If she doesn't come back, I'll have to look for her. Apparently this lodge has always been her home. She should be attached to this location even if she no longer has ties to Redge. I don't know how people like Candice and Redge get together in the first place. I suppose they remain together for company.

Having moved into cabin eight, Feston started to feel at home in his surroundings. He obtained supplies from the restaurant and lived in his cabin. He didn't trespass by entering other rooms at the restaurant or other cabins.

While ravens chattered overhead, he followed a lane. It took him to the mine. This is the Uinta mine I've heard so much about, he said to himself as he stood in the cavernous entranceway.

Removing a lantern from a ledge, he lit this lantern and started walking slowly into the tunnel. The lantern's pale, yellow light flickered along rock walls and roughly hewn beams. Hanging from some beams, there were metal, breastplates and helmets in addition to mining equipment such as pickaxes and shovels.

The air was cool, stale and damp. Water seeped from breaks in rock walls. Fes had not expected the tunnel to be so large and long. It came to a section where there was sand on the floor along with clay. Tendrils of water, moving down the walls, formed a pool before seeping into crevasses. On dry ledges along a wall, across from the pool, there were particularly large, pottery jugs used to store water. Looking around at the jugs and pond, along with crudely cut beams and rock walls, Feston said to himself, this is the Uinta mine I've heard so much about. It once contained only gold. Now these damp walls hold haunting stories of a mine worked by Spaniards followed by Brigham Young and the Mormons. This place has also had a grip on the Kellar family. More recently, I've been caught in its legend. Once people get involved with this place, they don't seem to be released. The mine seems to hold people, tieing them to an haunting past. Now I'm here waiting for Candice to return. I wonder if the mine will be able to keep her, or will I be the last one caught and the only one left to tell the story.

Feston walked to his cabin. He rekindled the fire and perked coffee. He sat dawn and sipped the stimulating drink while he watched flames flickering in the fireplace. Candice decided to leave this place, he said to himself. Because she wanted to leave, maybe she'll never return. At one time, she decided to stay with Redge and live in her home at this lodge. I wonder if she wanted to leave the lodge or Redge— or did she want to leave both of them. If she had wanted to find me, she knew where I was camped beside the lake. Apparently she decided to abandon everything and everyone— including me. Since she had reasons for her departure, there's only a slim chance she will return. Just because I've found myself to be always thinking about her, I can't assume she has a similar interest in me. One-sided relationships, I suppose, happen all the time. Real, two-sided commitments are rare.

The next morning, Feston was cooking breakfast in his cabin when the door opened. Standing in the doorway, Candice said, "Oh, it's you."

"Sorry," replied Fes, feeling pleased to see her again and irritated by her apparent disappointment in seeing him. "Sorry I couldn't have been someone else. If you were hoping to see Redge, he isn't here. He left with his girl friend, Carol, and two other guys. I've waited here for you. I've made a list of what I owe you. I hope your disappointment in seeing me here won't be too great."

"You don't have to be so rude," she stated. She seemed to be withdrawn and downcast.

"Okay," he said. "Do you want some breakfast?"

"Yes," she answered.

"The coffee's ready," said Feston. "You can pour some for both of us. I'll serve sausages and scrambled eggs."

"Thanks," she said, smiling, "but I prefer them sunny side up."

"Good to have preferences," he replied. "Today the eggs are scrambled."

"You might not last long in the restaurant," she said while she poured coffee, filling two cups. She placed one cup on a table beside the chesterfield and kept a cup for herself. She sat on a chair beside the fireplace. Fes brought her a paper plate containing scrambled eggs and sausages. On the plate, there was also a plastic knife and fork along with some ketchup. "I put salt and pepper on the eggs," he said as she received the plateful of steaming food.

"Thanks," she said. "I don't think anyone has served me anything better. Looks like good cooking."

"Maybe cooking here is almost as good as at your restaurant—although there are no choices," replied Fes. He prepared a second plateful of food. He took this plate to the chesterfield and sat down. "Where'd you go?"

"Out west—to the coast," she replied. "I needed a rest and time to think things over."

"Then you decided to return to Redge," said Fes.

"No," she stated with her face paling. "I came back to my home—in spite of Redge and all the trouble. I'm pleased that he's gone. He has taken his girl friend and cronies.

At first I just didn't like him. Now I hate him so don't keep mentioning him."

"Okay," said Feston, relieved to hear she was no longer tied to Redge. "Who were you expecting to see when you came in here?"

"I didn't know what to expect," she answered. "I hoped it wasn't Redge."

"Are you sorry I'm here?" he asked too directly for his own comfort.

"No," she replied.

"Did I have your approval to stay at your lodge in your absence?" he asked.

"Yes," she answered.

"You didn't stay out west very long," he said. "That's a long way to travel for a short time."

"I didn't have much money and I stayed long enough to make a decision," she replied.

"You decided to come home to Redge," he said.

"Home to me is this place—in spite of Redge," she answered.

"I've made a list of what I owe you," he explained. "I started leaving cash then decided to just keep a list and pay you the rest o' the money when you got home."

"You don't owe me anything," she said.

"My groceries came from the restaurant," he explained. "I didn't go into any other rooms or cabins."

"That's okay," she replied.

"Redge told me he took all the money," he said.

"I'm not surprised," she said. "I'm surprised to hear he would talk to you."

"We talked before the fight," he said.

"What happened?" she asked.

"Your friend Redge…" said Fes.

"He's not my friend," interrupted Candice.

"I came here to see you and make sure you were all right," continued Fes. "You weren't here and Redge was waiting for me. With him, he had his girl friend, Carol, and two guys, Carl and Roy. I knocked over Carl and Redge with a chair then kicked Roy in the fly. I used Roy's gun to knock Redge's knife out of his hand. The blade flicked back and stuck in the side of Redge's face. Before I kicked Roy, he shot at me and the bullet just nicked my throat, leaving a scratch that didn't bleed much. The blond woman helped the men get into three trucks. The four people in their trucks drove away, hopefully never to be seen again around your lodge. Redge said he was taking all the money, leavin' you with debts and no deed."

Candice was subdued and looking down at the floor as Fes refilled her cup. He put the plastic knives and forks in the sink. The paper plates were dropped into the fire before he added a piece of wood to hold down the paper.

After refilling his cup, he sat on the chesterfield. "Fortunately," said Feston, "I owe you money."

"You don't owe me anything," stated Candice. "You're the only person who has helped me. I don't have much money and the lodge is in debt. But maybe—probably—without having Redge around, customers will return. He argued and fought with everyone."

"You can really pick them," added Fes.

Annoyed, Candice replied, "I almost picked you."

"Oh, thanks," said Fes. "I get an almost and Redge…." Fes checked himself before he said too much.

"You'd be almost likeable if you wouldn't keep mentioning the one person I have reason to hate," stated Candice.

"Well," said Fes, "you're luckier than you think because I owe you some money."

"That's another thing you could stop saying," she answered. "You don't owe me anything. You're welcome to stay here as long as you wish. You have already greatly helped me. You've driven away Redge and the others."

"Did you ever wonder why I came here?" he asked.

"No," she said with a smile crossing her face. "I don't think about you at all."

"Well, your father sent me," said Feston.

"What are you talking about now?" she asked. "You don't even know my father."

"He's Cliff Kellar and he left this lodge because he thought he might kill Redge or get killed by him. Cliff warned me to watch out for Redge and his knives."

"Did my father send you here to get rid o' Redge?" asked Candice, completely astonished.

"No, not really, although he would've thought that was a good idea," answered Fes. "I suppose your dad figured keeping Redge around was your decision and…." Noticing the clouded look on her face, Fes said,

"Your father thought he had interfered enough—and so have I."

"How is dad?" asked Candice.

"He isn't well so he wanted me to give you a few things," said Fes. Candice looked down again. "The things he asked me to give to you are in my truck," added Fes as he stood up. "I'll get a package that was to be given to you."

Fes left the cabin. He walked to his truck, removed the haversack and carried it to the cabin. Giving the bundle to Candice, he said, "This is from your father."

She started opening the bag. Fes poured more coffee before sitting down again on the chesterfield. Candice had an entranced look on her face while she held the deed in one hand and rolled nuggets in the palm of her other hand.

"Your father has sent you the deed to this land," explained Fes. "He said the deed includes the lodge and mine. The nuggets came from this mine. Your father paid me with nuggets. I was to deliver these messages. I also delivered a pack of nuggets to Zackery Tomkins who was, at an earlier time, your father's partner and your mother's husband."

"Dad has really helped me," exclaimed Candice. "At times like this we find out who our real friends are. I've spent too much of my time with people who aren't my friends. In the future, I'm only going to be with people who are my friends. I must visit my father." Her eyes were watery. "I've heard about Zackery Tomkins. My mother left him then later left my father."

"There's one more thing Cliff sent you," said Fes. "He wanted me to tell you that precious stones, such as diamonds and rubies, had been extracted from jewelry. These stones were hidden in pottery jugs at the mine."

"There's only water in those pots," replied Candice.

"Cliff was definite about this," countered Feston. "He said there are diamonds and rubies in pottery bowls at the mine."

"We'll have a look," said Candice. "First I'm going to put this bag in the safe. I'm going to get something out of the safe and give this thing to you. You've earned it. Afterward, we'll check the pots in the mine." Candice stood up and, walking toward the door, she said, "Thanks for breakfast. Do you want to be a cook at the lodge?"

"Thanks for the offer," replied Fes. "However, you're the best cook."

They walked to the restaurant. Fes waited in the restaurant while Candice took the haversack to a room beyond the kitchen. When she returned she was holding a necklace consisting of a medal on a leather strap. "This is for you," she said, giving Fes the necklace. "The medal is from the Lewis and Clark Expedition. For a long time, this medal was stored in the mine. My father gave the medal to me. Now it's yours. You've earned it."

"Thanks," he said, accepting the necklace. He put the leather strap around his neck then started examining the medal. "I admire Lewis and Clark along with many of the other people on that expedition," exclaimed Fes.

"I wanted the right person to get that medal," said Candice, "and you're that person."

"I'll take great care of it," replied Fes. "I really appreciate this gift."

"Now we are going to the mine," stated Candice.

"So you think I'm the right one?" asked Fes while they walked toward the mine.

"Yeah, but don't get carried away," she replied.

The mine had the same forbidding, haunted presence with stale, damp air and rock walls that were wet with tendrils of seeping water. "This mine intrigues me," said Candice. Her words echoed and gradually lost themselves in the murkiness. The lantern's light flickered across beams and rocks. When this light danced across large, pottery bowls, Candice said, "The old pots only hold water used for drinking or washing."

Tipping the vessels gradually, Feston and Candice drained water out of one then the other three. "If my father said there were jewels in these bowls, he was mistaken or the diamonds and rubies were stolen a long time ago."

"Cliff wanted you to have these things," said Fes. "Can we take them to your lodge?"

"They're heavy," replied Candice. "I suppose they were made that way so people wouldn't steal them."

"We could carry one at a time," observed Fes. "Cliff wanted me to make sure you got these things."

"Okay," she agreed.

Working steadily and carefully, Candice and Feston took the bowls to her living room in the lodge.

Looking at the large, damp bowls, Candice said, "I don't really agree to having these things in the lodge. My father seemed to think they contained jewelry. You think I should have these old, water vessels. Considering all the gold you brought me, I suppose I can tolerate a few old pots."

"I've carried out my instructions," said Fes.

"You have done all you came here to do," added Candice.

"Yes," he replied. "I've been so busy delivering messages for Cliff Kellar, I've almost forgotten what my own life was like."

"You actually had a life?" asked Candice smiling.

"Yes, surprisingly," he said.

"That's a real surprise to me," she said. "You're going back to work?"

"Yes," he replied. "As I mentioned earlier, I'm a writer—sort of a newspaperman, working out of San Francisco. With the gold Cliff paid me, I'm goin' to build a log home beside the San Joaquin River. That's close enough to the newspapers in San Francisco."

"You were paid to do what you have done and now your work here is finished," she said. After looking down for a moment, she looked at him directly and asked, "What about me?"

"With the money your father has given you, you can put your lodge back into business," said Feston.

"I'll need help to run the place," she observed. "My father hired good help. He was lucky. Maybe I should do the same thing he did and hire you to help me run the lodge."

"I have work I'm doing in San Francisco," he replied.

"Nothing has changed that plan?" she asked.

"Just you," he replied.

"Oh, just me," she said. "Does that make any difference?"

Fes gazed around at his surroundings and the pots. He felt surprisingly cornered. He said, "I just remembered something and I'll be back." He stepped out of the room. For the first time, he was faced with the full difference that Candice had become for him and he found the sensation overwhelming. The difference was so large he was unsure of how to refocus his new situation. He hadn't experienced such a situation previously and was awed by the size of the difference Candice Kellar had come to make in his life.

"Feston," shouted Candice. "Are you leaving?"

"No," he answered, shocked by the enormity of what he had just realized. "There's no leavin' at this stage," he said. Walking back to cabin eight, he said to himself, I wonder when my attachment started with Candice Kellar. Was it at our first meeting or was I always included with the people who have become drawn in to the legend of this mine in the Uintas? Can we sort out one piece from the others or is everything too connected? The mine attracted the Spaniards, followed by Brigham Young and the Mormons. The Kellar family came next, then I was caught. I'm held now by this place because I'm completely tied to Candice Kellar and she is at home only with this mine in the Uinta Mountains. God must use gossamer strands of spirit to tie people—and places—together. However, we also have our own decisions to make. I can see things more clearly now. I always could think more clearly, or grasp life better, when I'm outside in the forest or wilderness. I know now that I can't leave.

Feston returned to the lodge. Seeing him enter her living room, Candice asked, "Forget something?"

"No," he replied. "I now know what I'm doing. I'm just remembering. Maybe the mine in the Uintas, and its legend, included me right from the beginning. I just didn't fully realize what was happening until now. Usually, when I do a newspaper article, I remain the messenger."

"Having discovered that you are part of this place, what are you going to do?" she asked.

"We'll run the lodge," he said.

"How do you plan to do that?" she inquired.

"We'll get married, then run the lodge," he said.

"When did you decide to do this?" she asked.

"I don't think I decided," he replied. "Today, I understood how things were."

"I can tell you how things are," said the resonant, malicious voice of Redge Osburn. He held a pistol as he stepped through the open doorway. Carl and Roy followed him. They had guns pointed at Fes and Candice.

To have these people break in on Feston's life, just as he fully understood it, infuriated him. Angrily and foolishly, he picked up a jug and was going to throw it when pain seared his arm as a bullet was shot through his muscle. The jug crashed onto the floor, exploding into chunks. Fes grasped a piece and hurled it at Carl's face, forcing the next shot to hit the ceiling. A second hurled chunk of pottery hit Roy's forehead, sending a stream of blood flowing across his face.

Fes found himself facing the barrel of Redge's gun just before Candice's scream caused the barrel to turn toward her. Fes sprang forward, shooting his fist into Redge's throat. He staggered backwards, dropping his gun. He was clutching his throat and gasping when Fes picked up the gun. He fired at Carl, hitting him in the shoulder. Carl's gun dropped. Roy's gun was thrown away as Fes aimed his gun at him.

The blond woman stepped through the doorway. She was shocked to see Fes holding a gun while her three friends were moving toward the doorway. "Load them into the trucks again," said Fes to the woman. "If I

see them again, I'm going to take a
shot at you."

She turned away sharply and was
followed by the three wounded men.
To Candice, Fes said, "That scream
saved my life."

"You saved our lives," she
replied. "Watch them and make sure
they are leaving."

Fes and Candice stepped outside in
time to see the last of the trucks
turn onto the road and move out of
view. "I don't think they'll come
back again," said Candice. "Those
people will turn against Redge and
he's had enough."

"We are lucky to be alive," said
Feston. "There's a mess to clean up
in there."

They returned to the living room.
"One of the first things I want to
do," said Candice, "is visit my

father and bring him back here to look after him."

"That's a good idea," said Feston. "We can hire a nurse if we need one."

After Candice had bandaged his arm, Fes picked up a piece of pottery. He was about to throw it into a garbage can when he saw a sparkling object lodged in the edge of the broken pottery.

The shining stone loosened after he tapped it with a second chunk of pot. "This thing's a diamond," exclaimed Fes. "Your dad said jewels were in the pottery bowls."

Fes gave the object to Candice. Turning the glittering stone between her fingers, she said, "It's a precisely cut diamond. Precious stones—diamonds and rubies—have been used for grit, or temper, during the making of pottery for the large pots. Just as my dad said, there's a fortune inside these bowls. With this money, we can look after my father and also take care of our lodge in the Uintas. I'm staying home and you have come home. Until today, you didn't realize you were a part of this place. We will rebuild the lodge and make the mine a place for visitors. You have found a story that took you into itself and it is the legend of the Uintas."

About The Author

Daniel Hance Page is a freelance writer, specialized in environmental and North American Indian issues, with four previous books published and numerous others being written. His books depict the history and culture of the United States and Canada with authentic stories that are spiritual as well as inspirational and are also filled with action, adventure and travel.